Total Reflexology

for the Hands

Total Reflexology
for the Hands

Work your way to wellness and relaxation

Barbara and Kevin Kunz

FALL RIVER PRESS

This book is part of the *Total Reflexology for the Hands* kit
and is not to be sold separately.

Fall River Press
122 Fifth Avenue
New York, NY 10011

ISBN: 978-1-4351-2362-5

Printed and bound in China

1 3 5 7 9 10 8 6 4 2

Contents

Introduction

YOUR HEALTH IS IN YOUR HANDS!

Reflexology has provided positive steps toward better health for the millions of people around the world who use it daily. Reflexology techniques apply pressure to the hands, nourishing the body with soothing signals. Whether you're using hands-on techniques or self-help tools such as the reflex ball, the pressure you're creating will give you a feel-good feeling. And feeling good is something you can practice!

Triggering the positive impacts of reflexology is easily within reach. With creative and easy ways to interrupt stress, reflexology surrounds enthusiasts with opportunities to use its techniques throughout the day. By applying a systematic program of pressure techniques, you tap into pressure sensors in the hands that act together with the entire body to enable you to move through the day. These same sensors contribute to the body's physical level of tension. Interrupt this tension enough and your body will revitalize itself. The successful reflexology experience allows you to take a break, resetting your body and providing a mini-vacation for your hands.

Reflexology also provides the ability to target specific concerns, such as health problems or injuries. By tapping into the reflex areas on your hands, you can become empowered to take charge of your body and the way you feel. The more you do, the bigger effect you'll have on your body.

Our client Jane, for example, had chronic asthma that caused her to wake up in the middle of the night unable to breathe, and she had become desensitized to most medications. We applied reflexology to Jane's hands, focusing on the adrenal gland reflex area, and gave her self-help tools she could use herself at home. Soon Jane could sleep through the night. Best of all, she was now in control of her own health, and could even use reflexology as a preventive measure against health problems for her two teenaged daughters. Jane's family's sense of well-being and quality of life was enhanced by low-cost, easy-to-use reflexology techniques.

You too can find health in your hands . . . starting now!

The use of reflexology, often handed down from generation to generation, has grown into a tradition in countries around the world. Many of today's reflexology techniques and theories stem from time-honored traditions dating back thousands of years. While it may seem natural to rub a tired hand or stubbed toe, evidence points to reflexology work as a therapy utilized by ancient physicians. Egyptian pictographs dating from 2350 B.C.E. carved into stone at the Tomb of the Physician at Saqqara depict scenes representing a form of reflexology. In the Medical Teachers Temple at Nara, Japan, built in A.D. 790, bronze statues of seated Buddhas have special symbols cast into their hands and feet that are thought to reflect reflex areas. Chinese, Indian, and other ancient cultures show evidence of reflexology practices as well.

As it was handed down through the ages, reflexology use and techniques ebbed and flowed. Today's reflexology came about as physicians of the late 1800s were trying to explore how the nervous system worked by using needles, pressure, the application of heat or cold, vibrations, and other techniques. The physical responses to these stimuli came to be viewed as reflexes, which led to the development of stimulating reflex areas on the hands and feet to impact specific parts of the body. Reflexology was also gaining a foothold in Asia, where hands-on work, self-help tools, and cobblestone paths were all in common use by the late 1900s.

In 1938, American physiotherapist Eunice Ingham was the first to fully develop and describe reflexology in a written work, *Stories the Feet Can Tell*, which outlined a system for applying pressure to the feet for expected health results. Many American and European hands-on reflexology systems resulted from Ingham's work, and more ideas have been incorporated into it over the years.

Today, people are drawn to reflexology use worldwide. Items such as pronged balls and sandals and electric hand and foot massagers can be purchased in almost every country. In Singapore, you can even see your own reflexologist at the reflexology kiosk at the mall. In Taiwan, tourists come from across Asia just for specific types of reflexology services that are offered by one of the region's many practitioners. China alone has more than five million reflexologists.

In ancient times, Octavian noted that Marc Antony rubbed Cleopatra's feet at dinner parties. In the modern world, Princess Diana had foot reflexology three times a week. In 2004, her letters to her reflexologist sold at auction for £19,400 ($38,100).

Parks in Asia are full of health-seekers walking on specially designed "reflexology paths," which simulate cobblestones and stimulate your feet when walked upon. So common are reflexology paths, hardly a condominium complex in Malaysia or Singapore is built without one. In Germany and Austria, reflexology paths are made with rocks, sticks, and mud. Cobblestone paths and portable cobblestone mats are becoming more and more popular in the United States, especially in the Northwest.

HOW REFLEXOLOGY WORKS

The pressure techniques of reflexology applied to the hands and feet trigger a relaxation response in the body. Triggering this relaxation response regularly throughout the day breaks up patterns of stress, and when these patterns are interrupted enough, the body is conditioned to function better. Like a successful exercise program, a successful reflexology style includes strategizing how often, how long, and how much technique is applied. As a user of reflexology, you will have to find the combination that works for you.

Reflexology's potential to relax the body and influence well-being is supported by scientific research. Some seventy controlled studies document positive results from reflexology work with disorders ranging from dysmenorrhea (discomfort during menstruation) to toothache. Positive effects have been experienced from all types of reflexology work, whether they're used on the hand or on the foot, done manually or with a tool, performed by another or practiced on yourself. Studies from around the world have shown proven results when using reflexology to improve digestion, help to regulate insulin in diabetics, help kidney function, lower blood pressure, lessen the pain and duration of childbirth, relieve the symptoms of chemotherapy, recover from surgery more quickly, and reduce spasms for multiple sclerosis patients. Reflexology has been shown to help ease depression and insomnia, and has even alleviated restlessness and wandering in Alzheimer's patients. Where you begin is up to you!

REFLEX AREAS

Reflex areas, shown on the chart and gloves in this kit, are targets for techniques. Getting to know the reflex areas will help you better obtain your health goals.

Reflexology is the systematic, organized application of pressure techniques to the hands and feet, and the reflexology chart provides a map of where to apply these techniques to get results.

The reflexology chart mirrors the body. The fingers and thumb reflect the head and neck, while the thumbs include the pituitary gland and thyroid. In between are the body's central organs and musculoskeletal structure. The left side of the body is mirrored on the left hand, while the right side is reflected on the right hand. As you go, pay attention to which parts of the hands feel stressed, and see if this mirrors the corresponding parts of your body.

Look over the reflexology chart and glove. If the part of the body you'd like to affect is listed, this reflex area is your starting place for technique application. For more specific health concerns, see Chapter One: Reflex Areas. This chapter will give you specific techniques you can use to affect the relevant reflex areas on yourself or someone else. As you become more skillful at focusing the right technique on the right reflex area, you'll notice that it takes less time to be effective.

Bolster your efforts by also learning techniques for general relaxation. An overall sense of relaxation will advance your progress with a specific health concern. Overall sessions by someone else (which can be found in Chapter Four) provide even further relaxation. Consider trading sessions with a reflexology buddy or seeking professional services. Finally, supercharge your efforts by simply relaxing and enjoying the reflexology experience.

SETTING A GOAL

Just as a bite out of an apple is a step toward health, every application of reflexology's techniques takes a step as well. Focusing on a goal, however, will allow you to be better able to target your concern and get results. Once you see results, you'll be motivated to do more reflexology. Success will breed success as you reach one health goal and move on to another.

For each technique in Chapters Two and Three, you'll find sidebars that give you specific instructions on how to use that technique to achieve your goals.

Our asthmatic client Jane, for instance, had the goal of being free of the asthma attacks that would wake her during the night. After learning the simple self-help technique, Jane was able to control her attacks and breathe more easily within three minutes of applying it. Fortified by results, Jane increased her efforts by applying the technique throughout the day. Soon she had accomplished her goal.

As you choose a goal or goals, consider the following: Are you seeking to trigger an overall relaxation response, rejuvenate hands, or focus on the health benefits of a reflex effect? If overall relaxation is your goal, you'll want to apply techniques to the whole hand. If rejuvenating hands is your goal, focus in on the areas that feel stressed. If you're seeking to impact a health concern, you'll want to target the relevant reflex areas. Once you've decided on a goal, decide to get yourself there!

CHOOSING THE TECHNIQUES THAT ARE RIGHT FOR YOU

Set the stage for success by choosing the reflexology techniques that are right for you. The right technique matches you: the amount of effort you want to make, your available time, and your likes and dislikes. Self techniques, which include using the reflex ball and your own hands, can be found in Chapter Two. As you try out the techniques, keep the following in mind:

Do you like it? Follow your fancy: use a technique you like. A good indicator will be whether or not you are able to find the time and energy to do it. Choosing a technique that appeals to you will make you want to do it more often, allowing you to more easily work the technique into your routine and get results. Enjoying your reflexology work will also release the feel-good hormones that are beneficial to your body.

Does it match your energy level? Reflexology techniques should be relaxing, not taxing. In general, if you try a technique and it seems like a lot of work, it may not be the one for you. Pick a technique that matches your available effort. If you're tired after a long day, for example, you may want to choose a technique that requires less energy.

Experiment with combining different techniques and trying new tools to find the type of reflexology you like. Feel free to create a technique that works for you!

FINDING TIME

Just as with any exercise, you'll want to do reflexology enough to prompt a change. The more you apply reflexology techniques, the more you interrupt stress. The more you interrupt stress, the more you trigger the body's natural repair system. Frequency, duration, and intensity (how often, how long, and how much) are the keys to being successful in reflexology. Every time you apply pressure to your hands, you are creating positive change.

If finding time is a problem, try choosing a reflexology technique that you can do while doing something else, such as watching television, using the computer, commuting on mass transit, or traveling as a passenger in a car. Decide on possible opportunities in which you'd have time to use reflexology, and pick a technique that fits.

Set up your reflexology possibilities in advance. Place your reflex ball anywhere you may be with a few minutes of free time: at your easy chair, at your desk, in the glove compartment, or inside your handbag or briefcase.

Using an electric tool such as a massaging wand can save you both time and effort. Results will be more generalized, but over time consistent use will lessen stress.

This worked well for our client Ed, who was plagued by pollen for years until he kept golf balls handy to use to affect his allergies.

Consider setting aside time to do reflexology every day. Ed, for example, used a reflex ball technique on his hands at each meal, three times a day. Get into the habit of integrating reflexology into your routine. Stack enough of these good habits together, and things will change for the better.

MAKING IT WORK

Getting results is all a matter of focused effort: your goal partnered with the right technique, the right reflex areas, and the right amount of time. Your reflexology success derives from a reflexology style that fits you. After you've determined what you want to accomplish, picked a technique, and found the opportunities to apply it, all you need to do is stick with it! More than anything else, regular technique application leads to successful use of reflexology.

In our more than twenty-five years of practice, we have noticed that it is those who do self-help or see their reflexologist regularly who see the biggest results. Being consistent with your reflexology program will not only help you maintain well-being, it will also help you when you need it most. Our thirteen-year-old niece was injured in a riding accident when her fingers were intertwined with the reins of a horse that took off running. Three fingers were in danger of paralysis, or even amputation. She credits the practice of daily self-help reflexology techniques throughout her convalescence with regaining the use of these fingers.

When reflexology becomes a part of your life, it's easy to recognize the possibilities of reflexology and remember to use it. Our client Jane, who had originally come to see us for asthma attacks, found herself in the emergency room with her daughter, who was experiencing extreme abdominal distress. For various medical reasons, no painkiller was administered during their five-hour wait for a diagnosis and operation, and Jane was able to draw on her reflexology experience to calculate where to press her daughter's hand to ease the pain.

APPROPRIATE USES OF REFLEXOLOGY

An important part of reflexology theory is deciding when to use reflexology and when not to use it. Never use reflexology techniques to work directly on a cut or bruise; any part of an injured hand; an ingrown nail; or a rash.

Do not work on a reflex area that is overly sensitive, and make sure not to overwork a single part of the hand. If a part of the hand feels bruised or tender to the touch, it may be overworked. Let it rest for a few days. When you begin your work again, work lightly and for a shorter amount of time.

One can make an assessment of the stressed parts of the body using reflexology, but there is a difference between an assessment and a diagnosis. Never use reflexology to diagnose critical issues involving an individual's health. Reflexology provides input, but it should not constitute the basis for your actions. Follow standard first aid or a medically recommended response first.

Finally, self-help tools are just that: instruments used to work on oneself. Never use the reflex ball, or another reflexology tool on someone else. There's no way to judge the impact of an instrument unless you yourself are receiving its impact.

AS YOU GO ALONG . . . USING REFLEXOLOGY

Both you and the recipient of your reflexology work will become adept at changing techniques to achieve the results you are seeking. As your work progresses, continually consider the effects it has. What exactly do you consider a benefit of your work? As one client commented, "I suddenly realized I could turn my head when driving to look at the traffic behind me." Effects can be subtle. Is the individual sleeping better? What other indicators of change can you see?

You are seeking just the right ingredients to most effectively and efficiently get results. Which areas you are targeting, as well as how much pressure to apply, how long to apply pressure, and how frequently you are applying pressure, will vary from situation to situation. The right formula—how much pressure is used and how long to apply it—gets results. Here are some things to keep in mind as you go along:

When applying techniques to yourself, use the gloves to home in on reflex areas or to find out which parts of the body are stressed. For more sensitivity, remove and gloves for an overall session.

Find the comfort zone. How much pressure you apply should always be within your comfort zone. Be aware of how the technique feels to you. You should be thinking, "That feels good." If there is a feeling of sensitivity, it should be a feeling of "it hurts good" rather than "it hurts bad." Discontinue work that "feels bad." If you're working on someone else, ask him or her "How does that feel?" as you go along and make sure you are working within his or her comfort level. If you aren't, ask, "Do you want me to go on?" When you proceed, make sure you proceed with respect for his or her comfort level.

If you are working on children, be aware that young children often do not have the words to express their reactions to your work or have the same response to pressure application that adults do. While an adult will respond with an expression of pain, a child will squirm as if to escape. (Some may leave at this point if you don't quickly soften your approach. Children are harsh critics.) When asked "Does that hurt?" they may say "No, it feels funny," or "No, it tickles."

Pick up the signals. It is a basic tenet of reflexology that pressing on the hand will cause an effect throughout the body. It is also true, however, that in applying reflexology techniques to the hand, you are applying pressure to hand! As you will probably notice, the person you are working on will react as you go through your reflexology session. In addition to asking your reflexology buddy how the technique feels, be aware of the nonverbal communication about your work. Keep an eye on the individual's face to gauge his or her reaction.

Get the "feel" of reflexology. As you work with the hands, consider what you're feeling under your working thumb or fingers. As you gain experience, you will also gain more and more of a sense of the "feel" for the surface of the hand. The patterns of stress you feel will create target areas for technique application. You will notice the change in the way the surface feels as your work progresses or as stress factors enter you or the individual's life.

ACTIVATING THE REFLEXOLOGY LIFESTYLE

There are many uses for reflexology. For some, reflexology offers the opportunity to spend special time with a family member or friend. For others, reflexology provides potential help for a health concern or happier hands and feet. For still others, reflexology offers a full range of such uses as maintaining physical dexterity and walking abilities, overall relaxation, and preventing illness.

Whatever your plans for reflexology use, consider not only how to do reflexology but also how to make it a part of your lifestyle. Plan for success by exploring your options in regard to techniques, time, and available locations for practice. On the following pages, we will focus on popular and successful reflexology techniques and give you the tools to incorporate reflexology into your life. But the goal of this book is to help you find a reflexology style that works for you. Just as decorating a room allows for personal creativity and expression, your reflexology style is your own. Use this book to design your reflexology experience. Fun, easy ways to feel better with reflexology are at hand!

Reflex Areas

1

BECOMING EMPOWERED TO ACHIEVE YOUR HEALTH GOALS is one of the biggest benefits of reflexology. This section will not only give you a place to begin your reflexology work, it will better acquaint you with which parts of your hands correspond to which parts of your body. After you find your health concern, use the diagrams at the bottom of that page along with the laminated chart and the gloves to pinpoint which reflex area to home in on to achieve results. Areas on right side of your body will be reflected on the right hand, and areas on the left side of your body will be reflected on the left hand. Keep in mind, reflexology should never be used as a diagnostic tool. If a particular area feels stressed, it simply means that the corresponding part of the body may be in the need of relaxing, not that there is something wrong with it.

In each section, you'll find techniques you can use to affect the desired reflex area. Techniques to use for yourself are shown in green, and techniques to use when giving someone else a reflexology session are shown in blue. After you find the technique that's right for you, apply it several times throughout the day to get results, and see your health improve.

Acne, commonly known as pimples or zits, are lesions of the skin caused by clogged pores. Pores get clogged when too much oil is produced by the sebaceous (oil) glands, often caused by our hormones. Pimples are most typically found on the face, neck, back, chest, and shoulders. Although acne is usually not a serious health threat, it can be a source of significant emotional distress.

Reflex areas: Adrenal glands, Kidneys

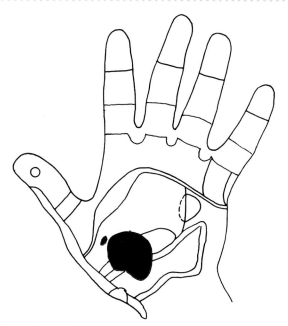
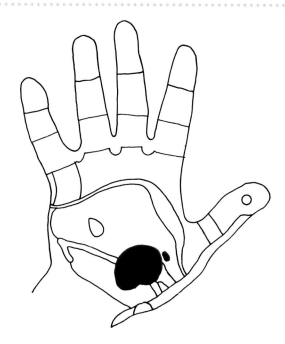

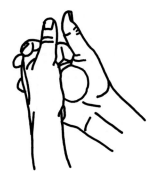

Reflex ball on heel of your hand below the thumb (p. 110)

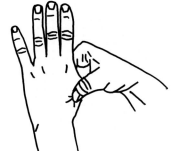

Pinch technique on the webbing between your thumb and index finger (p. 115)

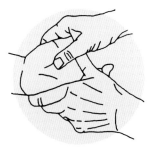

Thumb walk on heel of the hand below the thumb (p. 134)

ALLERGIES

Allergies are an overreaction of the body's defense mechanisms. These defense mechanisms, which normally protect against infection, can be triggered by certain foods, clothing fibers, pollen, and other materials. Use these techniques to help combat the symptoms of allergies; with continued work, you may also become less allergy-prone.

Reflex area: Adrenal glands

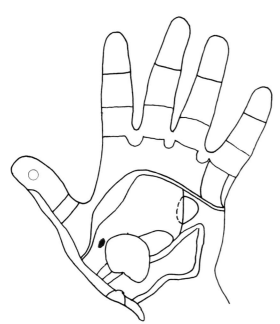 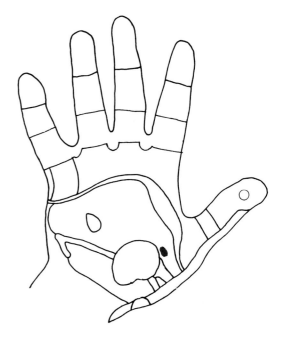

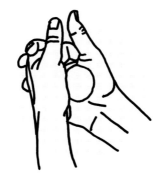

Reflex ball on your lower palm
(p. 110)

Single-finger grip on the heel of your hand below your thumb
(p. 114)

Single-finger grip on the heel of the hand below the thumb
(p. 123)

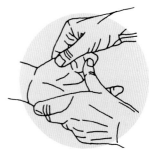

Thumb walk on the heel of the hand below the thumb
(p. 133)

ANXIETY

At some time or another, we've all experienced anxiety—a feeling of apprehension, worry, uneasiness, or dread, oftentimes about a future event. Constant or unreasonable feelings of anxiety are considered anxiety disorders. Try using reflexology the next time you're feeling anxious.

Reflex area: Solar plexus

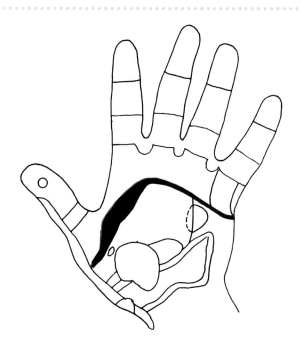 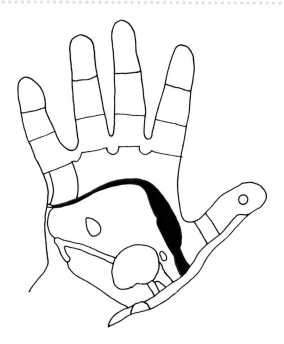

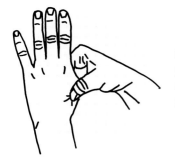

Pinch technique below your thumb and each of your fingers (p. 115)

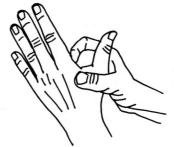

Reflex ball at the base of your thumb (p. 109)

Thumb walk on base of thumb (p. 134)

Single-finger grip in the webbing of the hand (p. 122)

ARTHRITIS

Generally, arthritis is a painful inflammation of the joints. Depending on the type of arthritis, it can be a continuous ache or pain in certain areas when moving, and normally affects those over forty.

Reflex areas: Adrenal glands, Kidneys

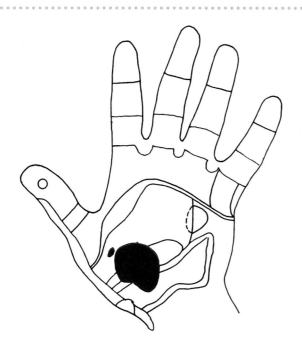
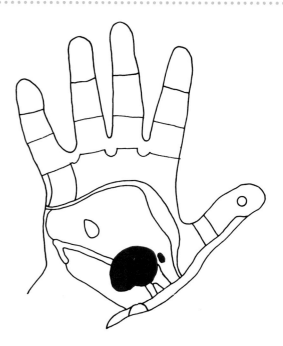

Reflex ball on heel of your hand below the thumb (p. 110)

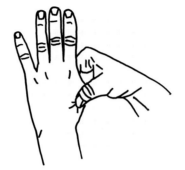

Pinch technique on the webbing between your thumb and index finger (p. 115)

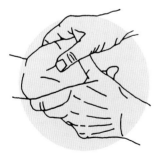

Thumb walk on heel of the hand below the thumb (p. 134)

Single-finger grip on the heel below the thumb (p. 123)

ASTHMA

Asthma is inflammation of the bronchial tubes that can make it hard to breathe. Associated with wheezing and coughing, asthma is often triggered by inhaling allergens such as pollen, mold spores, animal dander, or dust, and is the leading cause of chronic illness among children. Use reflexology to make asthma attacks less severe. Regular work in these areas can also help prevent severe bronchial tube inflammation (which leads to asthma attacks).

Reflex areas: Lungs, Adrenal glands

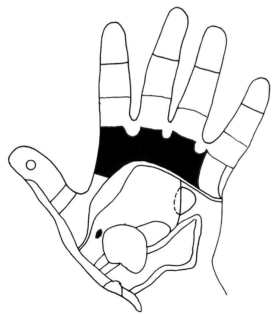 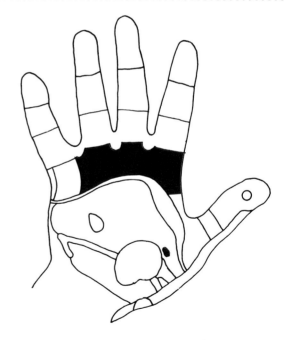

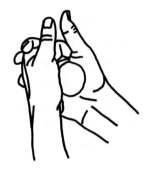

Reflex ball on the heel below your thumb (p. 110)

Single-finger grip technique on the heel below your thumb (p. 114)

Single-finger grip on the heel below the thumb (p. 123)

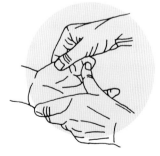

Thumb walk on the heel below the thumb (p. 133)

BACK PAIN

Most of us have suffered from back pain at some point or another. To use reflexology to help ease a sore back or combat postural fatigue, focus your reflexology work on the spine, the support structure for our bodies.

Reflex area: Spine

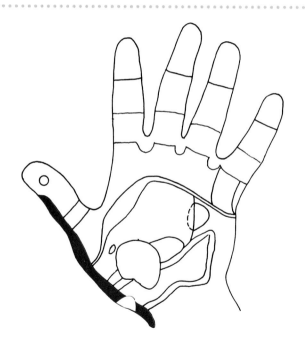
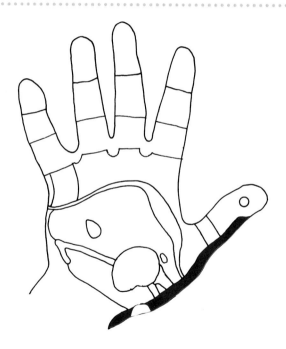

Reflex ball on the side of your thumb by the nail (p. 111)

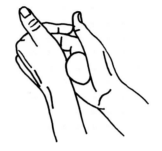

Reflex ball on the base of your hand (p. 111)

Thumb walk on the inside edge of the hand (p. 138)

CHRONIC FATIGUE SYNDROME

Chronic fatigue syndrome (CFS) is a debilitating medical condition with an unknown cause. Along with prolonged fatigue, sufferers often experience joint and muscle aches, sore throat, tender lymph nodes, and depression or other psychological problems. To help combat CFS, work the pancreas, adrenal gland, and brain stem reflex areas.

Reflex areas: Brain stem, Pancreas, Adrenal glands

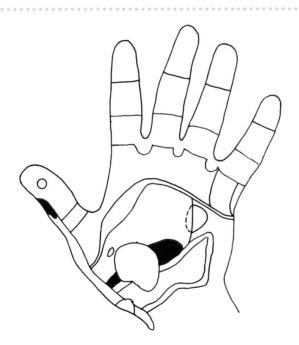 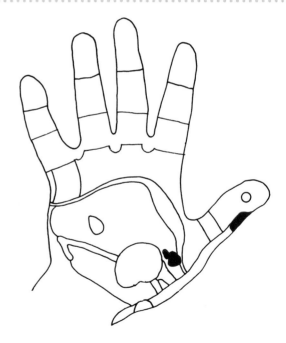

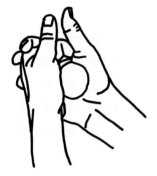

Reflex ball on the heel
below your thumb
(p. 110)

Reflex ball on the
edge of your thumb
by the nail
(p. 111)

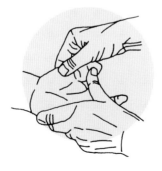

Thumb walk on the heel
below the thumb
(p. 133)

COLD SORES OR CANKER SORES

Whether it's a cold sore (a blister caused by the herpes virus) or a canker sore (an ulceration of the mouth or lips), reflexology can help get rid of these nuisances more quickly. Feel carefully for the most sensitive area on the thumb.

Reflex area: Face

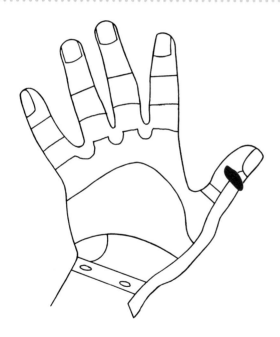 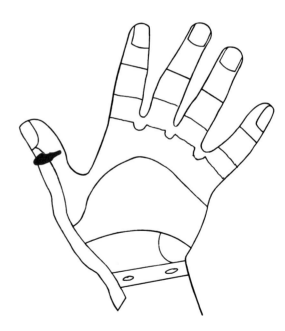

TECHNIQUES

Single-finger grip on your thumb below the nail (p. 114)

Thumb walk on the thumb (p. 132)

Find the sore spot: rub it out. That's an old saying in reflexology that especially holds true here. As you apply the single grip technique to the reflex area, consider what you feel. Reposition and press until you find the one spot that prompts you to say, "Ouch". This is your target. Hold your thumb in position on this spot.

CONSTIPATION

Constipation is a difficulty with bowel movements or unusually dry stool. It's most often caused by stress, not enough fiber or water intake, disruption of your regular diet, or pregnancy.

Reflex areas: Stomach, Colon, Small intestine, Pancreas, Gall bladder, Liver

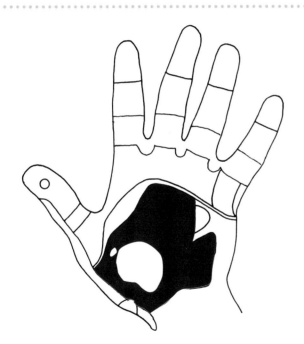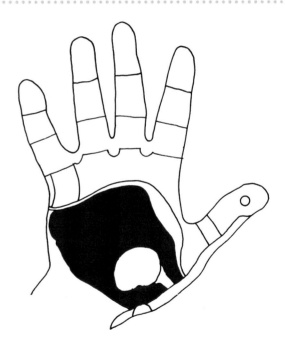

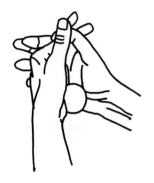

Reflex ball on the heel of your hand (p. 110)

Thumb walk on the palm (p. 134)

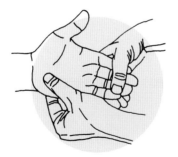

Thumb walk on the heel of the hand (p. 135)

DEPRESSION

Depression is a feeling of sadness or hopelessness that lasts for an extended period of time. Use reflexology to help ease depression.

Reflex areas: Solar plexus/Diaphragm, Pancreas, Adrenal glands

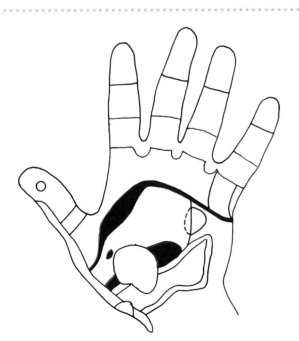 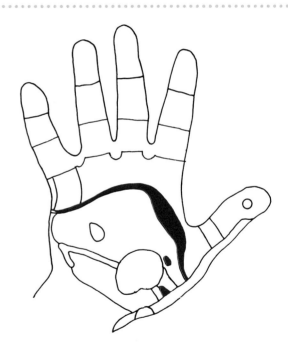

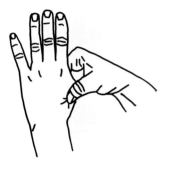

Pinch technique below your thumb and each of your fingers (p. 115)

Reflex ball on the heel below your thumb (p. 107)

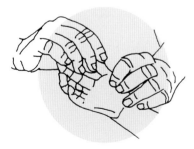

Single-finger grip on the heel below the thumb (p. 123)

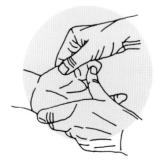

Thumb walk on the heel below the thumb (p. 133)

DIABETES OR HYPOGLYCEMIA

Both diabetes and hypoglycemia relate to blood sugar levels. Diabetes occurs when your body has trouble burning up sugar because of an insufficient supply of insulin (a hormone produced by the pancreas), and hypoglycemia is a deficiency of sugar in the blood. You can use reflexology to help with circulatory problems and blood sugar stability by working the pancreas reflex area.

Reflex area: Pancreas

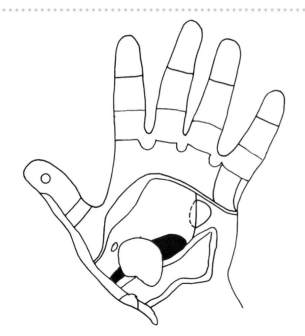 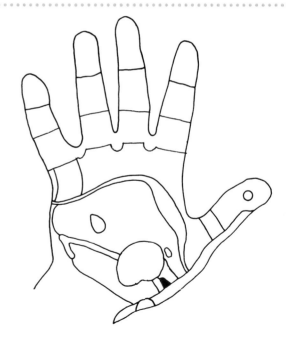

TECHNIQUES

Reflex ball on the heel below your thumb (p. 110)

Thumb walk on the heel below the thumb (p. 133)

There is potential to over-work this reflex area. (You know you've done so if this part of the hand is sensitive to light touch after your session.) If this happens, discontinue for a few days. When you apply the technique again, work for a shorter period, timing your efforts to see how much is too much.

DIGESTIVE TROUBLE

The digestive system is a complex series of organs that are easily disrupted. You can use reflexology to make digestion easier.

Reflex areas: Stomach, Colon, Small intestine, Pancreas, Gallbladder, Liver

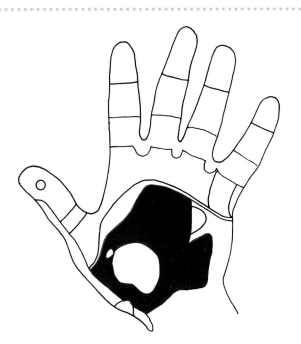
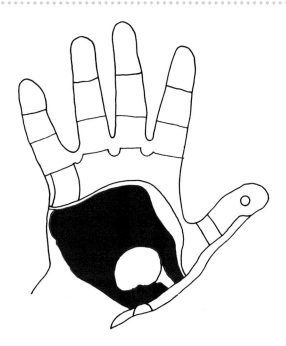

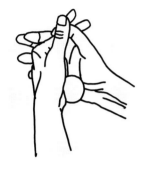

Reflex ball on your palm
(p. 110)

Thumb walk on the palm
(p. 134)

Thumb walk on the heel of
the hand
(p. 134)

DIZZINESS

Dizziness can result from any number of causes. Although it rarely signals a serious, life-threatening condition, dizziness can be disabling and incapacitating. Aging increases the risk of developing a condition that causes dizziness, one of the most common reasons older adults visit their doctors.

Reflex areas: Pituitary gland, Inner ear

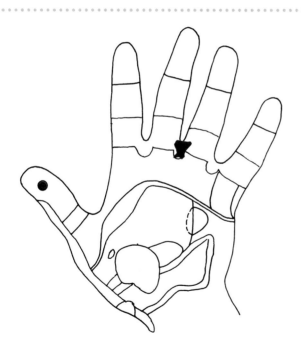
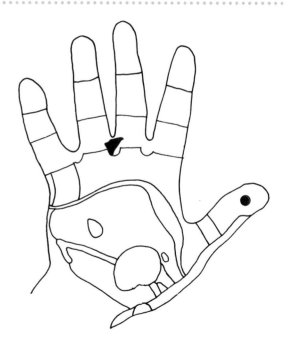

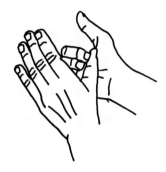

Single-finger grip on the center of your thumb (p. 114)

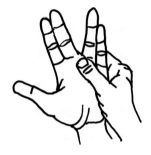

Pinch technique in the webbing between your fingers (p. 115)

Single-finger grip on the center of the thumb (p. 123)

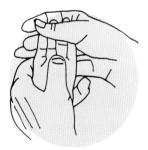

Single-finger grip in the webbing between the fingers (p. 122)

EARACHE

Most commonly found in children, pain in the ear is usually caused by infection and is most often a complication of an upper respiratory infection, such as a cold. Reflexology can help to lessen earache pain and make the infection go away sooner, and using these techniques regularly helps prevent chronic earaches in small children.

Reflex area: Ears

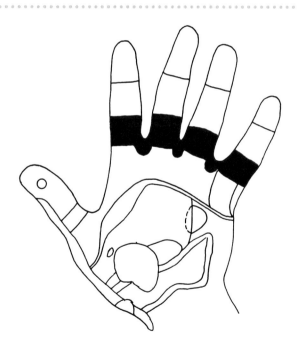
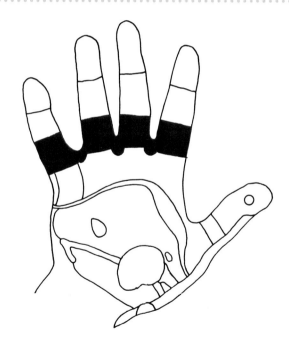

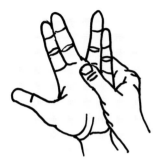

Pinch technique in the webbing between your fingers (p. 115)

Single-finger grip in the webbing between the fingers (p. 122)

Locate the sore spot and rub it out. Apply the pinch technique to the most sensitive spot. To help ease the pain of an earache, hold the pinch for 30 seconds.

EYE STRAIN

Reflexology work can help to ease eye strain.

Reflex area: Eyes

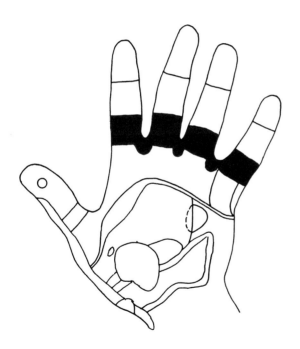
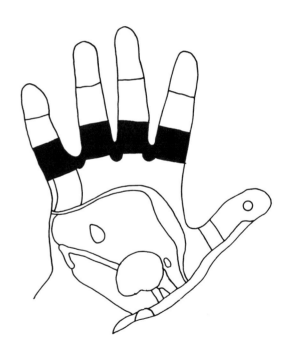

TECHNIQUES

Pinch technique in the webbing between your fingers (p. 115)

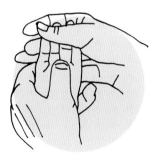

Single-finger grip in the webbing between the fingers (p. 122)

If eye strain is a common problem, apply the technique not only when your eyes feel strained but also periodically throughout the day.

FEVER

Most frequently a symptom of infection, fevers can leave you laid up for days. You can use reflexology to reduce a fever.

Reflex area: Pituitary gland

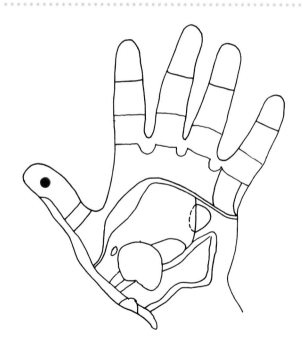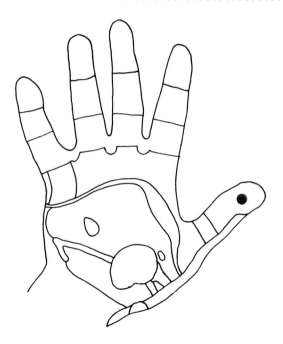

TECHNIQUES

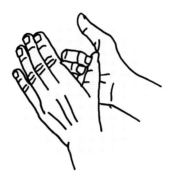

Single-finger grip on the center of your thumb (p. 114)

Single-finger grip on the center of the thumb (p. 123)

Frequency is the key to applying the technique for fever. Apply on and off pressure for 30 seconds every 15 minutes.

HANGOVER

The aftermath of drinking too much alcohol can result in headache, nausea, and other regrettable effects. To help ease this affliction, work various head reflex areas by using the reflex ball on your fingertips; affect the adrenal gland reflex area by rolling the ball on your lower palm.

Reflex areas: Head, Adrenal glands

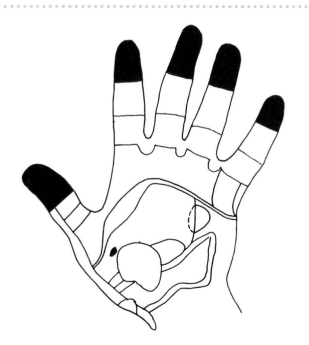 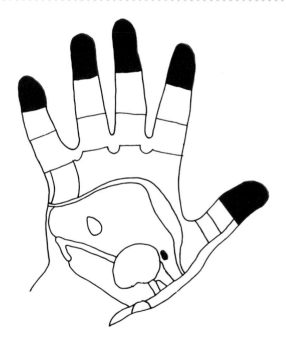

Reflex ball on the first segment of your thumb (p. 107)

Reflex ball on the heel below your thumb (p. 110)

Thumb walk on the thumb (p. 132)

Thumb walk on the fingers (p. 132)

HEADACHE

Headaches have many different causes, and more than 40 million people in the United States experience chronic headaches. Whether you get headaches frequently or rarely, you can help decrease their severity by using reflexology.

Reflex areas: Head, Solar plexus

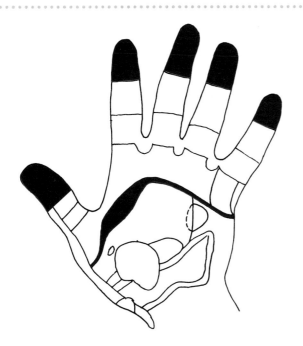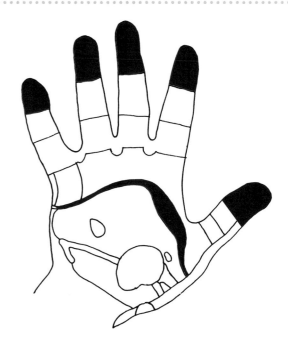

Reflex ball on the first segment of your thumb (p. 107)

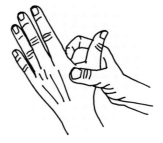

Reflex ball on the base of your thumb (try rocking the ball back and forth rather than rolling it in circles) (p. 109)

Thumb walk on the thumb (p. 132)

Thumb walk on the fingers (p. 132)

HEART PROBLEMS

The heart has a big job: keeping the blood circulating to carry nutrients, hormones, vitamins, antibodies, heat, and oxygen to our bodies' tissues as well as taking away waste materials. Focus your efforts on the heart reflex area, but also apply pressure to the solar plexus area, which will reduce stress and lower blood pressure, leading to a healthier heart.

Reflex areas: Heart, Solar plexus

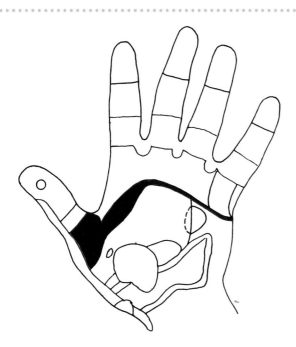
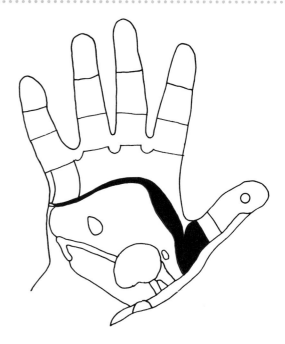

TECHNIQUES

Reflex ball on the base of your thumb
(p. 107)

Thumb walk at the base of the thumb
(p. 133)

Target the joint below the thumb, especially the portion toward the body of the hand.

HEARTBURN

Heartburn, or acid reflux, happens when acid from your stomach trickles up into your esophagus due to a valve in your lower esophagus opening too frequently or not closing tightly enough. Sometimes caused by a hiatal hernia, frequent heartburn is called gastroesophageal reflex disease (GERD), and can cause a variety of symptoms such as difficulty swallowing and damage to your esophagus. Reflexology can help lessen the frequency of heartburn.

Reflex area: Solar plexus

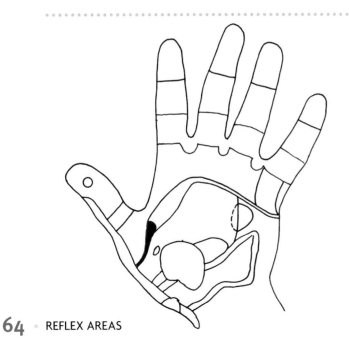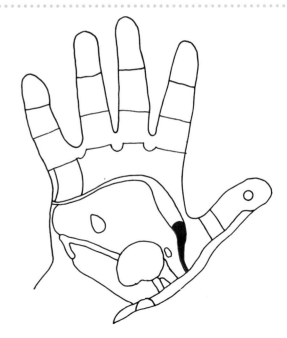

TECHNIQUES

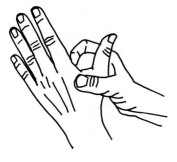

Reflex ball on the base of your thumb (rock the ball back and forth rather than roll it) (p. 109)

Single-finger grip at the base of the thumb (p. 123)

If you don't have a golf ball available, hold your hands as shown and exert pressure on the reflex area with the tip of your finger.

HEPATITIS C

Hepatitis C is the inflammation of the liver caused by blood infected with the Hepatitis C virus. An estimated 3.9 million Americans have been infected with Hepatitis C, and most (but not all) go on to have chronic liver problems. You can use reflexology to help keep your liver healthy.

Reflex areas: Liver, Adrenal glands

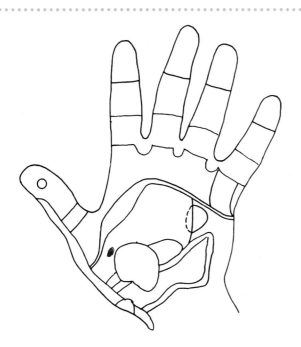 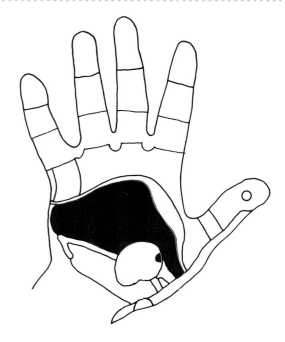

Reflex ball on your
lower palm
(p. 110)

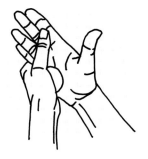

Reflex ball on your
lower palm
(p. 110)

Single-finger grip on
the heel below the
thumb
(p. 123)

Thumb walk on the
upper palm
(p. 133)

HIGH BLOOD PRESSURE

High blood pressure, or hypertension, is estimated by the American Heart Association to affect nearly one in three adults. High blood pressure increases the risk for kidney disease, heart disease, and stroke, some of the leading causes of death in the United States. To help lower your blood pressure, regularly use the reflex ball to work the solar plexus and the kidney reflex areas in the center of your hands.

Reflex areas: Solar plexus, Kidneys

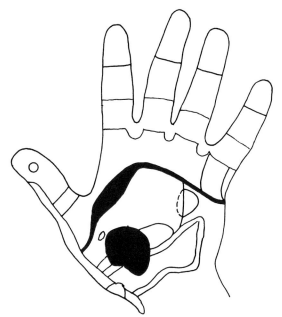 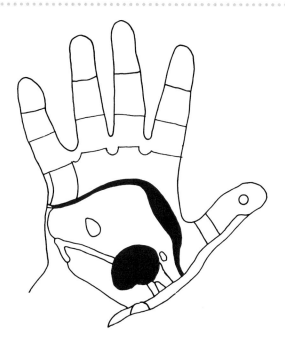

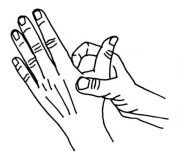

Reflex ball on the base of your thumb (rock the ball back and forth rather than roll it) (p. 107)

Reflex ball on your palm at the base of the webbing between your thumb and index finger (p. 110)

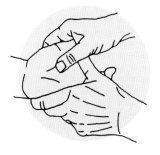

Thumb walk at the base of the webbing between the thumb and index finger (p. 134)

INCONTINENCE

Although it's often not talked about, incontinence (loss of bladder control) affects 25 million adults in the United States, according to the National Association for Continence. Reflexology work on the bladder as well as the brain stem can help lessen an incontinence problem.

Reflex areas: Brain stem, Bladder

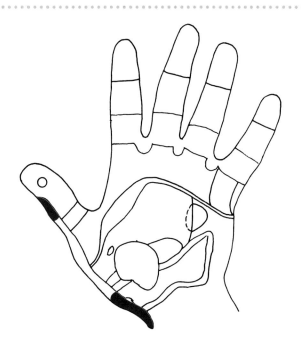 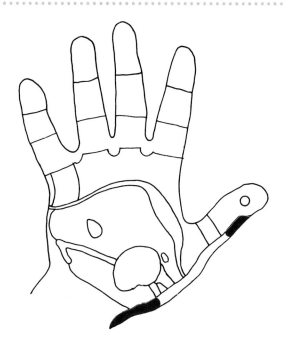

Reflex ball on the edge of your thumb by the nail
(p. 111)

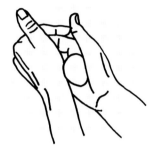

Reflex ball on the base of your hand
(p. 111)

Thumb walk on the inside edge of the thumb
(p. 138)

Thumb walk on the base of the hand
(p. 138)

INFERTILITY

Reflexology is in standard use at some fertility clinics, as many women believe it has helped them conceive. Even if you're not trying to conceive, hormones produced by the reproductive glands impact virtually every part of the body.

Reflex areas: Ovaries/Testicles, Uterus/Prostate

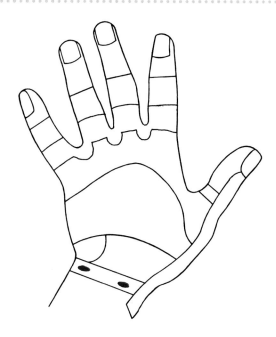 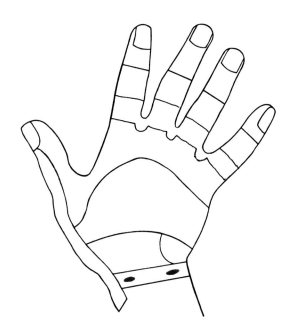

TECHNIQUES

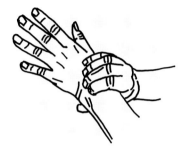

Rotate on a point on your wrist (p. 118)

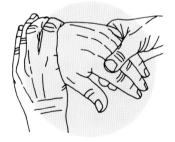

Rotate on a point on the wrist (p. 126)

Apply these techniques to pinpoint the reflex areas noted. Consider combining these with a whole hand workout from someone else for a bit of romantic hand holding and resulting overall relaxation.

INSOMNIA

Insomnia is the inability to fall asleep or stay asleep long enough to feel rested. Reflexology can help ease overall body stress, making it easier to sleep, and focusing specifically on the solar plexus reflex area can help with insomnia.

Reflex area: Solar plexus

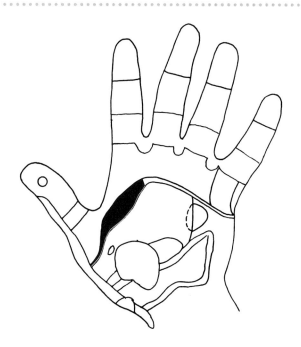 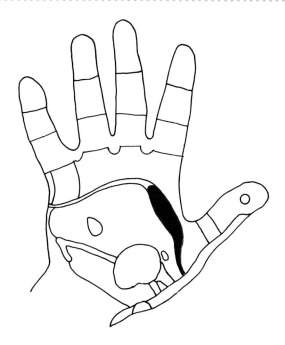

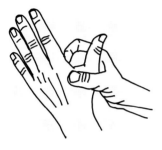

Reflex ball at the base
of your thumb
(p. 109)

Single-finger grip
in the webbing
between the thumb
and the index finger
(p. 122)

The solar plexus reflex area is
key to relaxation, but also consider
a whole hand workout by someone
else. Work by another, and to the
whole hand, is more relaxing.

The chief filters of the urinary system, the kidneys help regulate fluid in the body. Reflexology has been shown to improve blood flow to the kidneys, helping guard against kidney problems.

Reflex area: Kidneys

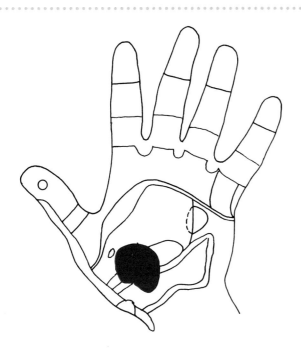
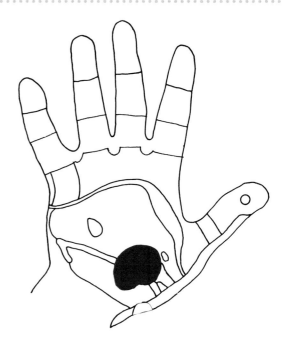

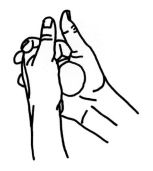

Reflex ball on your
lower palm
(p. 110)

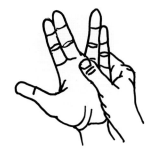

Pinch technique on
webbing
(p. 115)

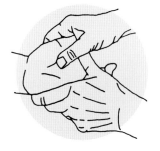

Thumb walk on the
lower palm
(p. 134)

MEMORY LOSS

Loss of memory can affect anyone, but is most often associated with the aged. Use reflexology to help improve your memory.

Reflex area: Head/Brain

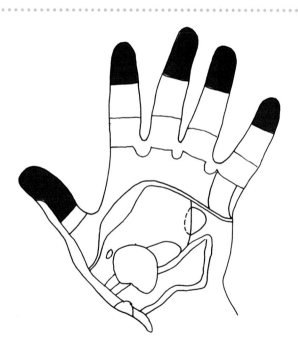
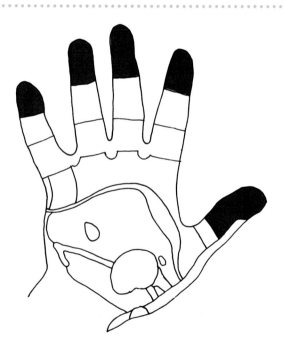

Reflex ball on the first segment of your thumb (p. 107)

Thumb walk on the thumb (p. 132)

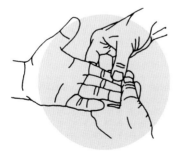

Thumb walk on the fingers (p. 132)

MENOPAUSE

This "life change" in women is usually accompanied by hot flashes, weight gain, feelings of weakness, and sometimes mental depression. Using reflexology can help ease these symptoms, especially hot flashes. Apply pressure to the palm's uterus reflex area by using the reflex ball on your lower palm.

Reflex area: Uterus

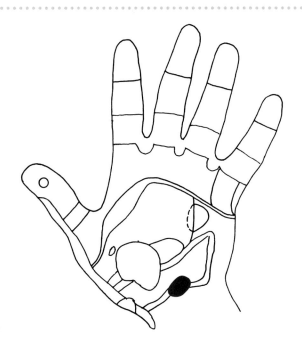 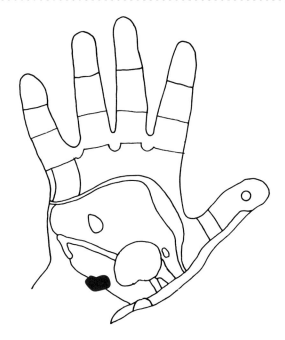

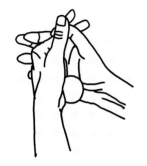

Reflex ball on your lower palm
(p. 110)

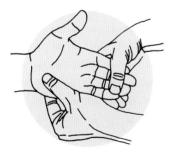

Thumb walk on the lower palm
(p. 134)

Frequency matters here. Stay ahead of hot flashes by working morning, noon, evening, and night. Or, you can apply the technique until symptoms subside.

MENSTRUATION

Painful periods not only reduce the quality of life for women, they sometimes make it impossible to go about daily life. Chronic cramping in the lower abdomen during periods even has a name— dysmenorrhea—and can worsen when you're under stress. With reflexology work, you can help ease the discomfort of periods.

Reflex areas: Uterus, Ovaries

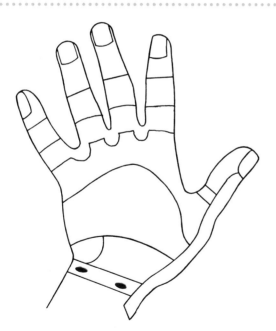

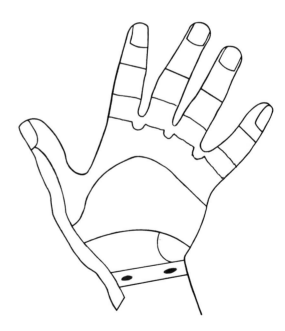

TECHNIQUES

Rotate on a point on your wrist (p. 118)

Rotate on a point on the wrist (p. 126)

Frequency (morning, noon, evening, and night) matters if you're working to ease discomfort during a monthly period. Or, you can apply the technique until symptoms subside.

MIGRAINE HEADACHE

Migraine headaches are chronic, intense headaches that can last up to 72 hours and are often accompanied by nausea or visual disturbances. These techniques can also help ease the pain associated with cluster headaches, trigeminal neuralgia, vascular disorders, and post-traumatic head pain.

Reflex area: Head, Tailbone

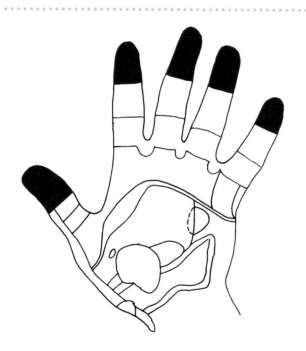 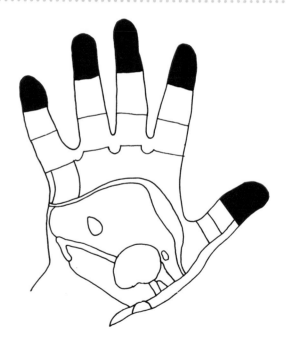

Reflex ball on the first segment of your thumb
(p. 107)

Modify the direct-grip technique by sliding the flat of your thumb down your finger while stretching your finger to the side
(p. 116)

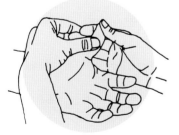

Thumb walk on the thumb
(p. 132)

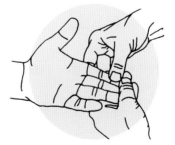

Thumb walk on the inside edge of the thumb
(p. 138)

PREMENSTRUAL SYNDROME

PMS is characterized by physical, psychological, and emotional disturbances brought on by changing hormonal levels after ovulation, normally ending with the onset of your period.

Reflex areas: Uterus, Ovaries

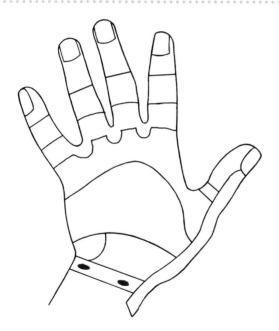
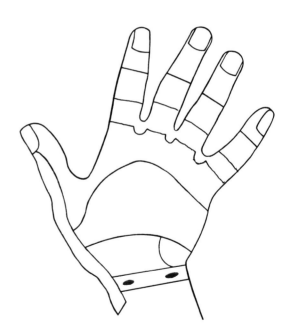

TECHNIQUES

Rotate on a point on your wrist (p. 118)

Rotate on a point on the wrist (p. 126)

Apply techniques throughout the month to the help avoid discomfort during your period. Make it a part of your day, applying the technique for a few minutes. Keying it to when you eat is an easy way to remember (breakfast, lunch, dinner). Get in the habit and stay in the habit.

SCIATICA

"Sciatica" is the term for lower back pain (around the sciatic nerve) that travels through the buttock and down one leg. The pain usually goes past the knee and may go farther to the foot, sometimes causing weakness in the leg muscles. To work the sciatic nerve reflex area, use the reflex ball on your lower palm.

Reflex area: Sciatic nerve

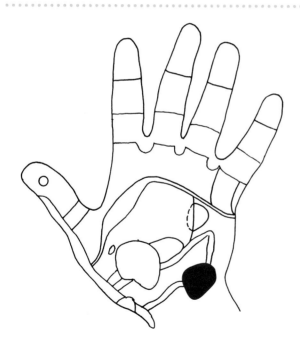
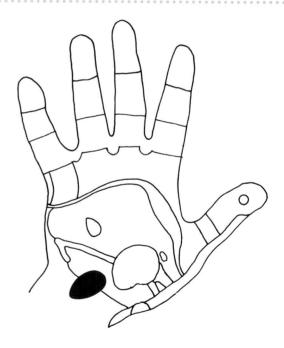

TECHNIQUES

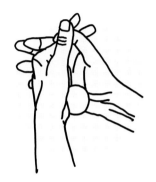

Reflex ball on your
lower palm
(p. 110)

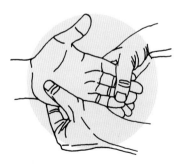

Thumb walk on
the lower palm
(p. 135)

As you roll the golf ball or
apply the thumb walking technique,
search out the most sensitive
spot for your focus.

SHOULDER PAIN

Minor shoulder problems often occur from over-exercise or simply normal use. Reflexology is an easy way to help ease shoulder pain.

Reflex area: Shoulders

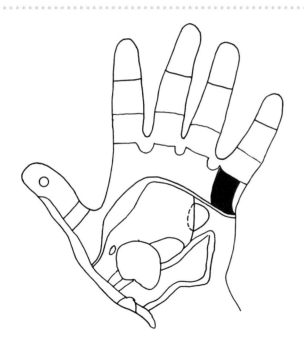 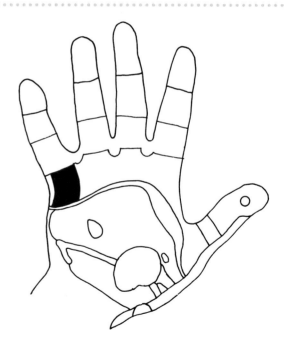

TECHNIQUES

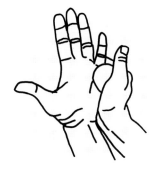

Reflex ball below your little finger (p. 109)

Thumb walk on the palm below your little finger (p. 135)

The find-the-sore-spot, rub-it-out rule applies here. Find the specific part of the reflex area that is most sensitive. Hold the golf ball or your thumb in place applying a constant steady pressure for 30 seconds or until pain subsides. Or, roll the golf ball or thumb walk through the reflex area.

SINUSITIS

Sinusitis is the inflammation of the tissue lining of your nose and other sinus passages. Often caused by a cold or allergies that lead to an infection, sinusitis can result not just in a stuffy nose, but in headache; neck pain; earache; pain in the teeth, jaws, and cheeks; and eyelid swelling.

Reflex areas: Sinus passages, Adrenal glands

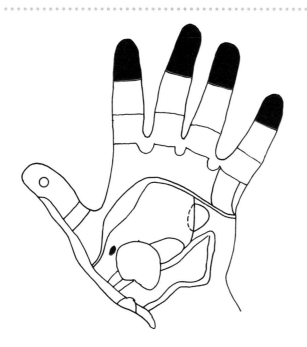
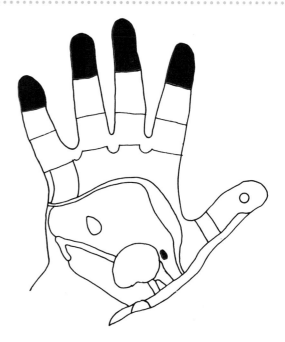

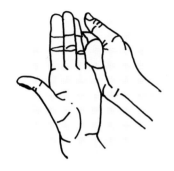

Reflex ball on your fingers (p. 108)

Single-finger grip on your palm, feeling for the most sensitive area (p. 114)

Single-finger grip on the palm (p. 123)

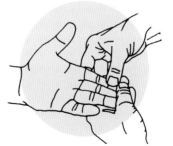

Thumb walk on the fingers (p. 132)

SORE THROAT

Most sore throats are caused by minor illness. Try using reflexology to ease this common occurrence.

Reflex area: Throat, Adrenal glands

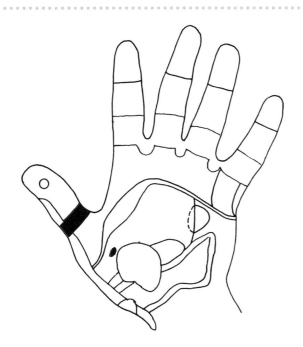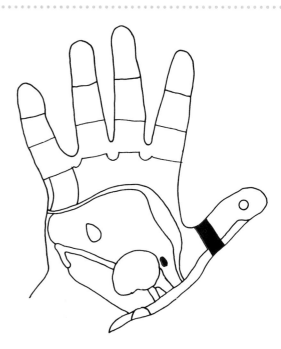

Reflex ball on the second segment of your thumb (p. 107)

Reflex ball on the heel of your hand below the thumb (p. 110)

Thumb walk on the thumb (p. 132)

Thumb walk on the thumb (p. 132)

STOMACHACHE

Many things can lead to an upset stomach, from eating too quickly to stress. Stomachaches can be made worse by smoking, stress, excessive drinking of alcohol, and certain medications.

Reflex area: Stomach

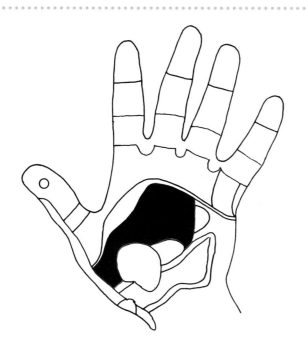 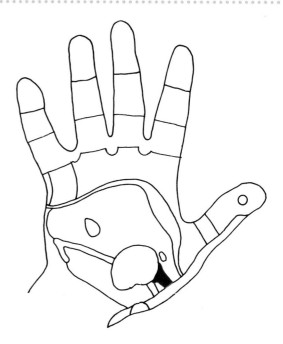

TECHNIQUES

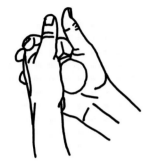

Reflex ball on the heel of your hand below your thumb (p. 110)

Thumb walk on the heel of the hand below the thumb (p. 134)

Apply the technique until the discomfort eases. If you frequently have stomachaches, stay ahead of the game by applying this technique several times a day, especially right after a meal.

STRESS

The American Psychological Association estimates that 75 to 90 percent of all visits to a doctor's office are due to a stress-related ailment.

Sometimes we can't escape stress, but reflexology can help.

Reflex area: Solar plexus, Adrenal glands

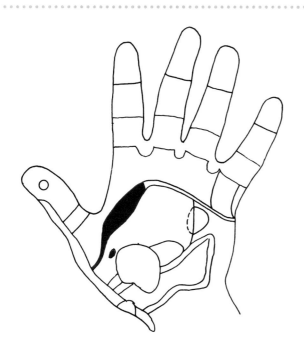
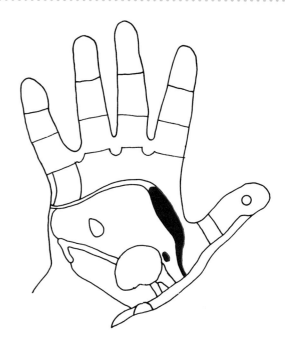

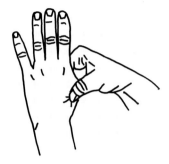

Pinch technique below
your thumb
(p. 115)

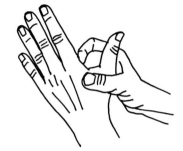

Reflex ball at the base
of your thumb
(p. 109)

Single-finger grip in
the webbing between
the thumb and
index finger
(p. 122)

Single-finger grip in
the webbing between
the thumb and
index finger
(p. 122)

ULCER

Usually caused by an infection, an ulcer is a sore in the lining of your gastrointestinal tract, made worse by the acidic nature of the stomach and by stress. Symptoms of an ulcer can include nausea, vomiting, pain in the abdomen, and bloody stool.

Reflex area: Solar plexus

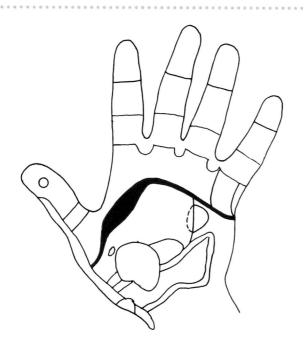 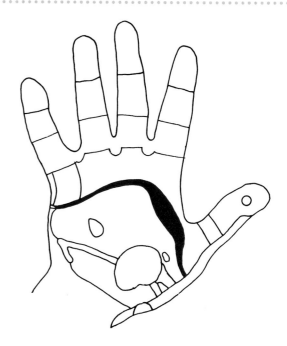

TECHNIQUES

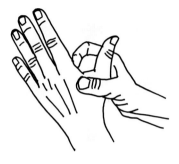

Reflex ball on the base of your thumb (rock back and forth rather than roll) (p. 109)

Single-finger grip in the webbing between the thumb and index finger (p. 122)

Find the sore spot and key in on it with your technique application. To ease pain, hold the golf ball or your fingertip in place for 30 seconds or until the pain eases.

2

FINDING A REFLEXOLOGY TECHNIQUE THAT'S RIGHT FOR YOU is essential to making sure that you get the results you want and having the motivation to keep it up. Get comfortable and work through all of the reflex ball techniques and manual techniques on the pages that follow to discover which ones work best for you. The hands are the most convenient site for reflexology work. They are easily accessible, which comes in handy when dealing with a chronic condition (such as hay fever) that needs a lot of continual work.

Initially, your hand may feel stiff or tight. You may not feel that much is happening. Perhaps you'll enjoy the experience immediately or maybe take a while to develop a feel for it, as you may not be accustomed to spending so much time with your own hand! To pique your interest, try this experiment. As you work, imagine yourself exploring a new sense, one seldom visited. Each and every pressure-sensing area of the hand awakens a feeling of control over one's health. Not only will you relieve the tension of the day and begin to relax, but you will gain a foothold on becoming less stressed in the future.

Reflex Ball

DON'T LEAVE HOME WITHOUT IT—the reflex ball, that is. At least, that was the opinion of a certain five-year-old, who insisted on turning the car around to go home for "his" golf ball. As the story was told to us, it was the first his parents knew about the child's use of a reflex ball technique to ease his migraine headaches.

This speaks to the ease of using the reflex ball and its great advantage in addressing health concerns. It's small. It's portable. It's easy to use. And the hands are always accessible. Such a combination provides plenty of potential for success. Frequency counts in reflexology, and using the reflex ball means being able to easily work every part of the hand with the pressure needed for results.

Using a reflex ball provides many benefits: improved circulation, happy hands, and a way to tap into the body's natural resources for wellness. A reflex ball strategy allows you to interrupt patterns of stress and compensate for hard-working hands. Relaxed hands make the whole body feel good, and practiced enough, reflex ball techniques will result in improved health and a lessened potential for stress-related illnesses.

What's Your Goal?

If your goal is a general relaxation response for your body, use a slow rolling motion with light pressure. Use as frequently as desired and for as long as it's relaxing. The reflex ball is easy to take with you, so it's perfect to use throughout the day to counter stress as it occurs.

If your goal is to rejuvenate your hands, focus on the specific part of your hand that feels tired, and apply the reflex ball to counter overuse. Use moderate pressure: enough to cause your hand to relax while still staying within your comfort zone. Use frequently to break up the patterns of stress and keep them broken up.

If your goal is to impact a specific part of your body and/or a specific health concern, the reflex ball is for you, thanks to its ability to target specific reflex areas coupled with the ease of frequent use. You'll want to use the reflex ball frequently enough to break up the pattern of stress. Give yourself time to learn the different reflex areas—some of which are pinpoint—and apply steady pressure.

In general, to use a reflex ball (which is simply a golf ball) cup it in your hand, press it against your other hand, and roll. Holding the ball in place is important both to keep it in control and effectively apply pressure, especially when targeting specific reflex areas. Be aware that it is easier to overwork an area with the reflex ball than with manual techniques. (Overwork has occurred when a touch to the area feels like a bruise.) Be conscious of your individual response to the pressure exerted by the ball, and choose a level of pressure according to your comfort level. If overwork does occur, let the area rest for a few days. When you begin again, use less pressure and/or work for less time to avoid future problems. While good for self-help, using the reflex ball to work on another person is not suggested.

Problems can result from the combination of the ball's hard surface and too much pressure, and it's hard to gauge the results of the applied pressure on someone else.

Ready to roll? Get out the reflex ball, sit comfortably, and pull on the reflexology gloves. Rest one hand in your lap, palm up, with the other hand on top and the ball in between. Roll the reflex ball between your hands, covering both the fingers and palms.

Take a break and wiggle your fingers to test how each hand feels. Go on rolling the ball between your hands, taking note of how long it takes to make your hands feel good and how long it lasts. Then establish a frequency for how often to use the reflex ball throughout the day.

Consider how different areas on your hand feel as you roll over them—what feels good, and what doesn't? If an area feels good, work it more to relax your hand. If an area feels stressed, the corresponding area of your body may need reflexology work. Compare the location of the stressed part of your hand with the reflexology chart on the glove. Think about whether this matches your own health observations as well as observations by healthcare professionals. A lower back or digestive stress pattern, for example, is pictured in the heels of the hands. To gauge your stress in this area, try rolling these parts of the hands, experimenting to see if

The reflex ball has a mind of its own! It even squirts out of our hands (sending our cats running for cover). The techniques in this chapter are designed for ball control.

you can make your lower back feel more relaxed. Try taking off the glove and rolling the ball on your bare hand to see if this works better for you.

Time yourself. Once again, notice how long it takes to make this area of your body feel better, and set a frequency (even if it's a general one) for using the reflex ball throughout the day. Develop a strategy for an all-day good feeling!

Pick out some target areas based on what feels good or on what health interests you'd like to pursue as indicated by the reflex areas on the chart. Use the instructions on the following pages to home in on these target areas. Once again, notice how long it takes to get that good feeling, and set a frequency (even if it's a general one) for rolling your hands throughout the day. Try keeping the reflex ball close at hand—on your desk, in the car, or by the TV; or take it with you in a purse or bag. And keep on rolling!

To better home in on your body's problem spots, try using the hands-on techniques in the next section.

THUMB

To work the thumb, hold the ball with your index and middle fingers, positioning it as shown.  Once in this position, pressing the ball with the thumb of your "working" hand controls the ball and creates pinpointed pressure. Now that you have a stable working surface, move your working hand to roll the ball across your thumb. Cover the length of the thumb with succeeding passes, repositioning your working hand as needed. Also try using the ball on the tip of your thumb.

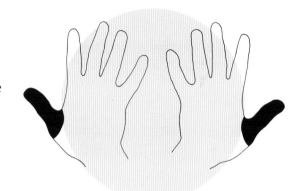

TECHNIQUE

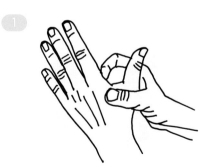

FINGERS

Cup the reflex ball in your working hand, wrapping your four fingers around the finger to be worked.  **1** The four fingers help to hold the ball in place and to create the desired amount of pressure. To generate more pressure, press with these fingers. To lessen pressure, loosen the grip of these fingers. Roll the ball over your index finger. Make succeeding passes until the length of the finger has been covered. Then continue with each remaining finger. **2**

TECHNIQUE

1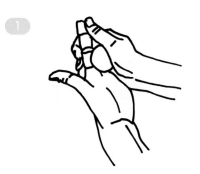

2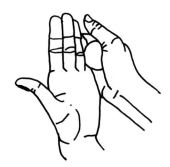

UPPER PALM

To work your upper palm, begin by cupping the ball in your working hand. Place the ball at the base of your thumb and wrap your fingers around it. 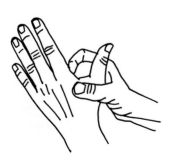 Roll the ball back and forth, covering the joint and adjusting pressure by pressing with the fingers of your working hand. Reposition the ball below the index finger. 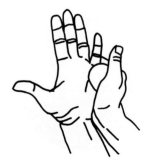 Roll the ball around the palm and into the trough between the knuckles and below your index and middle fingers. Again, lessen or increase pressure by adjusting the pressure of your working hand. Go on to work the knuckles below the middle, ring, and little fingers.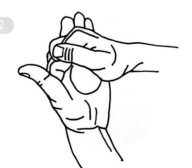

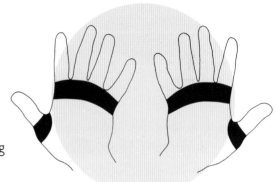

TECHNIQUE

LOWER AND CENTER PALM

The palms of both of your hands can be worked at the same time. Hold the reflex ball as shown, and roll it throughout the center of your palms, pressing with the fingers that are resting on the back of the hand to create more or less pressure. 1 Now try resting the ball in the heel of your hand below the thumb. Clasp your hands together, interlinking your fingers. 2 Roll the ball over this surface. Move on, positioning the ball lower on the heel of the hand and rolling here as well. 3

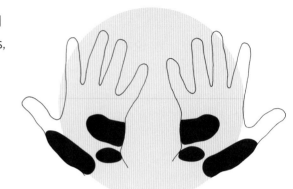

TECHNIQUE

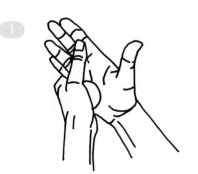

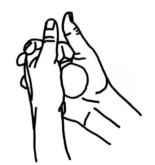

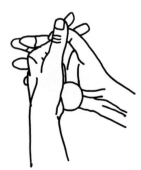

OUTSIDE OF THE HAND

Cup the ball in the palm of your working hand, wrapping your fingers around your thumb (but this time without your thumbs touching). **1** Roll the ball, pressing with the fingers to create the desired pressure. Reposition your hand and the ball to further work the fleshy edge **2** and outside of the thumb. **3**

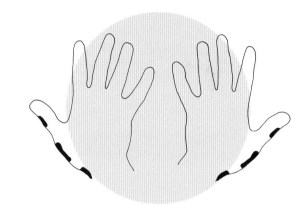

TECHNIQUE

Hands-On Techniques

GET TO KNOW YOUR HANDS with hands-on techniques. Learning manual techniques can take time, but there's nothing better for figuring out where your stressors are located. Tapping into the sensory-rich system of your hands allows you to feed messages of relaxation into the stress mechanism and gather direct feedback about what parts of your hands are stressed. Because you'll actually be able to feel the tension, manual techniques are an easy, straightforward way to reach reflex areas. So let's take a tour of hands-on techniques.

What's Your Goal?

* If your goal is to achieve an overall relaxation response, you'll want to apply techniques to your whole hand.

* If your goal is to bring life back into your tired hands, consider your level of tension. Flex your hand and decide what parts feel stressed, tight, or even painful. (In fact, your entire hand may feel stressed.) Target the stressed areas with the techniques in this section.

* If your goal is to influence certain body parts and functions, these hands-on techniques allow you to target specific reflex areas. To create a reflex effect, give yourself time to learn the different reflex areas, some of which are pinpoint. Time your efforts and set a frequency to get results.

Slip on a glove and leave your other hand free to do the work. To apply a complete reflexology session to your hand, the goal is to make contact with each area on the reflexology glove. Use the techniques on the following pages to make contact and exert pressure, going through all the reflex areas on one hand and then the other. As you go, consider what each area feel likes and compare the reflex areas on the first hand with their corresponding areas on the second hand. If an area on one hand is more sensitive than its counterpart, that side of your body may be under more stress than the other.

Take care not to overwork your "working" hand by applying techniques longer than you're comfortably able. Switch to another technique if your hands feel strained. Also, some techniques may cause your fingernails to dig into the skin. Keep an eye out for fingernail marks on your hands, and trim your nails or modify your grip as neccessary.

To apply these techniques to someone else's hands, see Chapter 3: Techniques for Others

SINGLE-FINGER GRIP

Single-finger grip techniques are an easy way to work many parts of the hands. Place the tip of your index finger in the center of the thumb.  Apply pressure several times. Also try this technique in the heel of the hand below the thumb by curling your index finger into this fleshy part of the hand. Your target is halfway along the long bone and slightly toward the webbing of the hand. Exerting pressure with the flat of the thumb works well in other parts of the hand, too. Give it a try by resting your thumb on top of the other thumb. Press. Reposition your thumb; press again.

TECHNIQUE

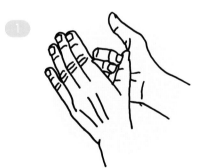

PINCH

The webbing of the hands provides a great opportunity to reach certain reflex areas that reflect body parts that are commonly stressed. Try this technique by placing the flats of your index finger and the thumb of your working hand in the webbing of your other hand. ① Press several times. Reposition your hand by placing the flats of your finger and thumb in another portion of the webbing and press again. ② Go on to try this technique on the webbing between each of your other fingers.

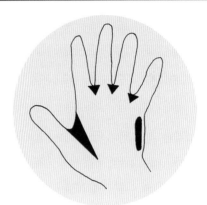

TECHNIQUE

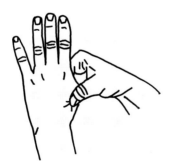

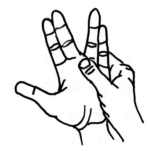

DIRECT-GRIP

Almost any part of your hand's palm can be worked with the direct-grip technique. Try applying pressure to various areas on your hand. Rest the flat of your thumb on the palm of your hand and press. Try moving your hand from side to side. (But be aware of the impact of your thumbnail on your palm.) Move on to other parts of your hand.

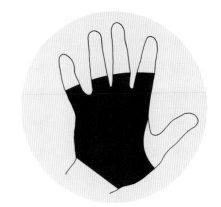

TECHNIQUE

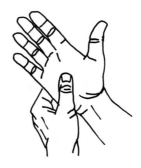

MULTIPLE-FINGER GRIP

For this technique, the tips of all four fingers are used to apply pressure across a wide area. Try this technique on your hand by resting your fingertips in each trough and exerting pressure. Try moving your hand from side to side and experimenting with other parts of your hand.

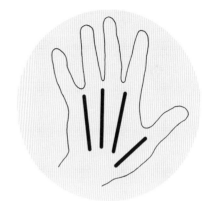

TECHNIQUE

ROTATING ON A POINT

To try rotating on a point on your hand, rest your fingertip on your wrist. Press gently with your working hand and move the other hand in a circle, first clockwise and then counter-clockwise.

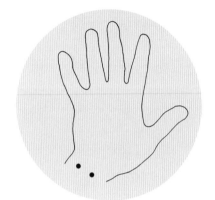

TECHNIQUE

Techniques for Others

THE FIRST RULE OF CREATING AN ENJOYABLE REFLEXOLOGY EXPERIENCE for someone else is to be in touch with the recipient's reaction to your work. What the recipient says and does are your cues to continue your work or find a better approach. As you work, ask "How does that feel?" If the answer is something like, "Good," or "It hurts a little, but feels good," then what you are doing is working—remember it for next time! If the response is "It hurts, and feels bad," use a lighter touch.

As you try the techniques and work the areas described in this chapter, you might notice that some people enjoy a particular technique no matter where it's applied, while others respond positively to certain techniques applied to particular reflex areas (use the gloves to figure out if the individual's pattern of stress matches a reflex area). Remember, not only will you want to adjust your target areas and techniques, you will also want to adjust your pressure level, the length of time you apply the technique, and how frequently you apply it to find the mix that's right for your reflexology buddy. You should always be aware of how the recipient is responding to what you do, and be ready to make adjustments as your work progresses or as stress factors enter the individual's life.

Grip Techniques

GRIP TECHNIQUES ARE QUICK AND EASY ways to use reflexology to lower overall body stress, ease tired hands, and target specific reflex areas. With grip techniques, you use your fingertip (or fingertips) to press a part of the hand, then move to a new place and press again. When paired with the reflexology gloves, they serve to create an uncomplicated and straightforward workout approach.

What's Your Goal?

* If your goal for the individual is a general relaxation response for his or her whole body, use a very light touch as you apply these techniques.

* If your goal is to rejuvenate the individual's hands, attempt to target the patterns of stress. Begin by using medium pressure, staying aware of his or her response. Try to find the proper amount of pressure to cause the hand to relax.

* If your goal is to trigger a relaxation effect in a specific part of the body, you'll want to make a focused effort: spend more time doing it, do it more frequently, and consider the level of pressure that's most effective.

Because we all know how to grasp something, there is no new method to learn for the grip techniques. Focus instead on experimenting with exerting different levels of pressure with the tip of your finger or thumb as you explore the techniques. See what level of pressure applied repeatedly most relaxes your reflexology buddy. Remember, always begin reflexology work on another by pressing lightly. Don't press with your full strength!

As you go, take note of what parts of your reflexology buddy's hands are stressed. If you're using the reflexology glove, note how these stressed areas relate to the reflex areas. Pick out some target areas based on which areas feel stressed or what health concerns your buddy would like to pursue. Use the techniques on the following pages to focus on these target areas, and maintain a steady pressure for a few seconds rather than pressing several times. Direct pressure such as this will create a painkilling effect in the corresponding part of the body.

Begin with the single-finger grip technique, in which your thumb will be working on the bottom of the hand with your fingers resting on top. After you've tried the single-finger grip you'll be ready for the multiple-finger grip. Here you'll be using all of your fingertips at once to apply pressure across a broader area of the hand. Finally, rotating on a point will show you how to pinpoint an area on your reflexology buddy's wrist.

Make sure your nails don't leave "chicken tracks" (our name for the impressions that nails leave on the hands). Take care not to overly curl your fingers when applying the grip techniques, and keep your nails trimmed, so you don't leave a trail of nail prints as you work.

SINGLE-FINGER GRIP TECHNIQUES

WEBBING OF THE HAND

With your thumb on the top of the hand and your index finger on the palm (or vice versa), press your fingertips together through the webbing between the fingers several times. **1** Experiment by moving your fingers to another place in the webbing and pressing with your thumb. **2** Does the webbing under your fingertips feel different in different locations? If so, take note of which areas are more stressed and work them next time. Also try this technique on the fleshy outer edge of the hand.

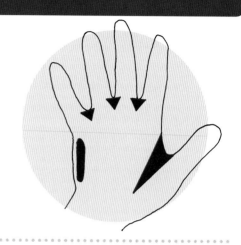

TECHNIQUE

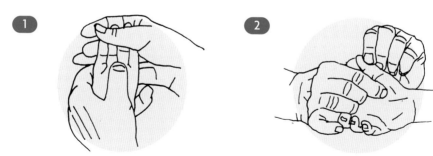

THUMB AND PALM

Use your holding hand to hold back the individual's fingers. With your working hand, rest your index finger on the palm of the hand and your thumb on the top of the hand. **1** Gently press several times with the tip of your index finger. (Try to avoid digging your fingernail into the skin!) Move on, using this technique in the center of the thumb. **2** Try using different amounts of pressure in different places on the hand and see how it feels to your reflexology buddy.

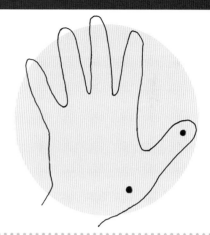

TECHNIQUE

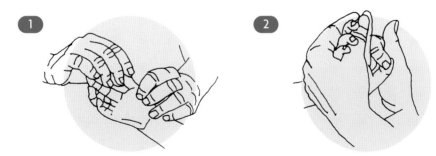

MULTIPLE-FINGER GRIP TECHNIQUES

PALM AND FINGERS

Hold back the fingers with your holding hand, and rest the fingertips of your working hand on the palm. **1** Press with multiple fingertips gently. Experiment with differing levels of pressure while avoiding digging your fingernails into the skin. Increase your pressure and ask your reflexology buddy how it feels. Now move on to a different part of the palm and continue to press repeatedly.

You can also use the multiple-finger grip on each finger. **2** Press gently with your fingertips, then a little harder as you ask your buddy how it feels. Try to get an idea of the person's comfort level. Proceed to each finger, gauging your buddy's response as you go.

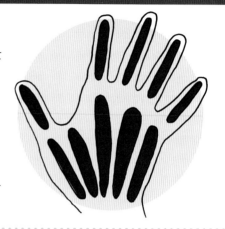

TECHNIQUE

BACK OF THE HAND

The multiple-finger grip technique is especially good for the back of the hand. With your thumb on the palm of the hand and your fingers together on top, find the areas between the long bones in the hand. Press gently several times as you move across the hand to each area. When you get close to the thumb move your hand to the other side and grasp from the front. **3**

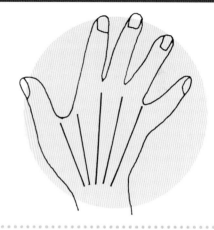

TECHNIQUE

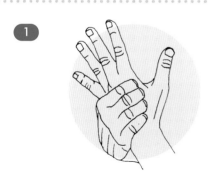

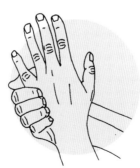

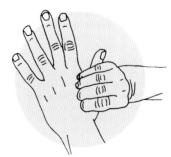

ROTATING ON A POINT TECHNIQUES

WRIST

While holding the hand in place top side up, place the tip of your index finger on the top of the wrist with your thumb resting on the bottom.  **1** With your holding hand, grasp the upper hand and turn it in a clockwise direction, drawing circles in the air. Then turn it in a counterclockwise direction. Pinpoint another area on the wrist and repeat. **2**

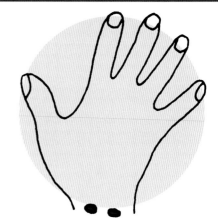

TECHNIQUE

1    **2**

Thumb- and Finger-Walking Techniques

"WALK" ALONG THE HANDS with these techniques, which provide precise pressure by using the edge of the thumb or fingers as they "walk." Thumb- and finger-walking techniques are designed to maximize efficiency and effectiveness in applying pressure to the hands. In reflexology, "efficiency" means covering a reflex area with the least amount of effort; "effectiveness" means hitting the points—being dead-on target in every reflex area. With a little practice, thumb and finger walking will be among your most useful tools in reaching these goals, because the interplay between the holding fingers and thumb will give you the ability to exert pressure on all of the varied surfaces of the hands.

Thumb walking is achieved by bending your thumb at the first joint (the one closest to the tip of your thumb), and then taking small "steps" with it across the hand. Pressure is increased or decreased by lifting or dropping your wrist, as this uses leverage to create pressure at the thumb's tip. Finger walking is

What's Your Goal?

* If your goal is to achieve an overall relaxation response, apply these techniques to the entirety of both hands using light pressure.

* If your goal is to bring life back into tired hands, take note of the stressed parts as you go. Work through each both hands, focusing special attention on these parts.

* If your goal is to affect certain body parts or to address health concerns, thumb- and finger-walking techniques allow you to easily target specific reflex areas. Use the reflexology gloves, and give yourself time to learn how to effectively apply pressure to individual reflex areas, some of which are quite small and can be difficult to pinpoint.

frequently used on the bony tops of the hand. Either one finger or all fingers work the surface. Like thumb walking, the basis of the finger-walking technique is the bending of the working fingers at their first joints.

Before you begin thumb and finger walking on your reflexology buddy's hands, give it a try on your own arm so you can get a feel for it first. Use the instructions that follow to practice thumb and finger walking.

Bend and unbend your thumb at the first joint while grasping it at the second joint to keep it steady. This movement is the basis of thumb or finger walking. **1**

Rest your hand on your leg and try this same move. Your thumb should "walk" forward. Continue to bend and unbend your thumb, taking small steps forward with each unbending motion. **2**

Now try practicing this technique on your arm. Rest your fingertips on the top of your arm with your thumb on your arm's underside. While keeping your fingers in place, bend and unbend your thumb against the underside of your arm. As you unbend your thumb, take a small step forward. Practice walking your thumb in a forward direction. Keep your other fingers in place until your hand is stretched uncomfortably, then reposition them, continuing to keep them in place as your thumb walks. **3**

Maintaining the position of your fingers, lower your wrist slightly. Do you notice that the tip of your thumb is now exerting more pres-

As you practice thumb walking, make sure you're only bending your thumb at the first joint! If you find that your thumb tires easily, you may be pressing with it instead of "walking" with it. Focus on creating leverage by dropping your wrist rather than pressing with your thumb. The same apples to finger walking.

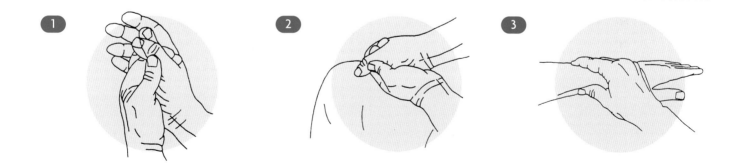

sure? Now drop your wrist lower. Your thumb should be exerting even more pressure. As you can feel, leverage is created by an interplay of the fingertips, wrist, and thumb tip. **4**

Practice the thumb-walking technique by walking along your arm. As you go, try to exert constant, steady pressure. This is most easily achieved by effective use of leverage as described in step 4. **5**

To finger walk, rest your index finger on the top of your hand, and work up the hand in between the bones, taking small "steps" while maintaining constant, steady pressure. **6**

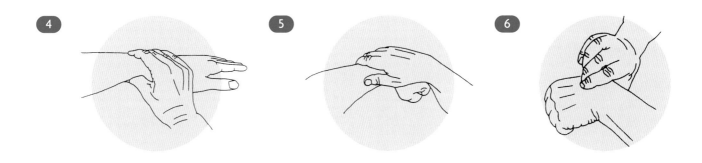

4   **5**   **6**

Take care not to overwork your hands by applying techniques longer than you're comfortably able. If your hands become tired, switch to another technique. Make sure to give yourself time to learn the techniques and how best to make the most of the physical effort expended. Though they may take a little while to learn, these walking techniques will become one of the most valuable tools in your reflexology arsenal.

Practice thumb and finger walking using the instructions that begin on the next page before you go on to the walking techniques that follow.

THUMB-WALKING TECHNIQUES

FINGERS

With your holding hand, stretch the fingers back, beginning with the thumb, so that the hand is open. With your working hand, rest your fingers underneath the hand and place your thumb at the base of your buddy's thumb. **1** Raising your wrist to create leverage as necessary, bend and unbend your thumb at the first joint to move it around the thumb. **2** Take small steps and exert constant, steady pressure. Proceed in the same manner with each digit. **3**

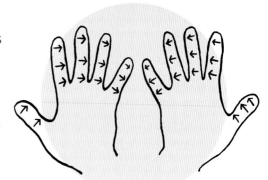

TECHNIQUE

UPPER PALM

While holding the fingers back with your holding hand, position the thumb of your working hand so that it rests on the bony joint below your buddy's thumb. **1** Now walk your thumb forward (away from the individual's thumb), making several passes. Move on to the bony joint below the index finger. **2** Work your way across the hand, working each joint as well as the trough between each finger. **3**

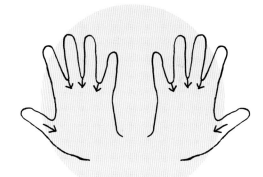

TECHNIQUE

1

2

3

THUMB-WALKING TECHNIQUES

LOWER PALM

To use the thumb-walking technique on the lower palm, begin in the fleshy part of the hand below the thumb. **1** With the fingers of your working hand resting on the back of the hand for leverage, walk your thumb down to the wrist. Reposition your thumb and make several passes, each time beginning at the padded part of the palm. **2** **3**

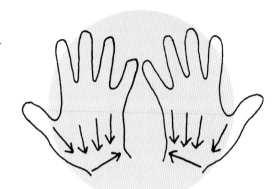

TECHNIQUE

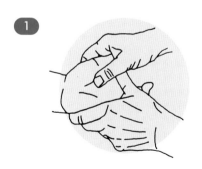

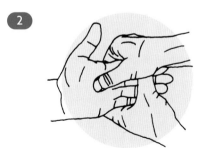

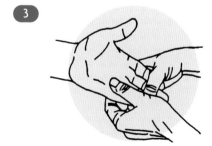

HEEL OF THE HAND

Hold back the fingers with your holding hand, and position your working thumb near the wrist. **1** Thumb walk toward the wrist, making a series of passes to cover the area. To work just above the heel, position your working thumb above the heel of the hand below the index finger. **2** Holding the fingers back, thumb walk down the palm. Reposition your thumb and make several passes.

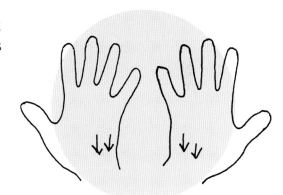

TECHNIQUE

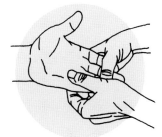

THUMB-WALKING TECHNIQUES

TOP OF THE HAND

The top of the hand is a bony surface with troughs that form convenient working paths for your thumb-walking technique. Rest your working thumb at the base of the fingers, **1** and thumb walk along each bony trough. **2**

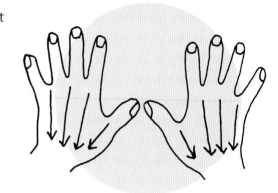

TECHNIQUE

FINGERS

Rest your buddy's fingers on the fingers of your holding hand, and use the thumb of your holding hand to hold those fingers steady. With your working hand, begin at the base of the nail ❶ and work your way across the first finger, ❷ bending your thumb at the first joint and taking small steps. Move your holding thumb as necessary, and continue on to each finger.

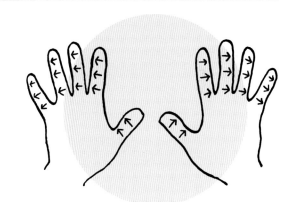

TECHNIQUE

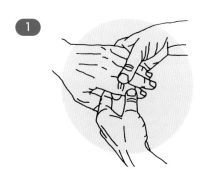

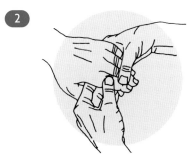

THUMB-WALKING TECHNIQUES

INSIDE OF THE HAND

To work the inside edge of the hand, first hold the thumb in a stationary position. With your working hand, use the thumb-walking technique to walk up the inside edge. **1** Reposition your hand as your thumb becomes stretched. Now go on to the inside edge of the thumb. **2**

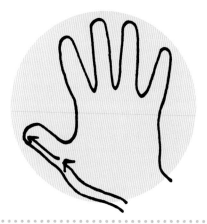

TECHNIQUE

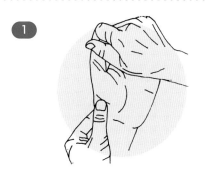

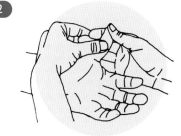

Desserts

JUST AS DESSERTS ARE A FAVORITE PART OF ANY DINNER, these "dessert" techniques may become the favorite part of a reflexology workout. These relaxation techniques are perfect for interspersing throughout a routine to ease

What's Your Goal?

* Desserts are created specifically to relax the hands. Try using them before you start a routine to get the hand warmed up and ready to be worked on.

* If your goal is to rejuvenate the hands, try using the desserts throughout a reflexology session to break up stress patterns and make the hands more comfortable. An all-dessert session will help breathe life back into those tired hands.

* Using desserts can help achieve your reflex-effect goals by providing an overall sense of relaxation. In addition, specific reflex areas can be affected when the dessert is applied in a particular region, such as in the lung press dessert.

Desserts are perfect for introducing your children to reflexology. (Not surprisingly, children love these desserts too!)

sensitivity, warming up the hand for hands-on techniques, or creating an overall feeling of comfort.

In general, the joints and other areas of the hand are moved in one way and then another to systematically create movement. Desserts can play an important role in mitigating tension caused by the day-to-day activities of the hands. By relaxing the hands and moving them in new directions, the desserts are perfect to use at the beginning of a reflexology workout to get your buddy ready for the rest of the techniques. Desserts are also a great way to give your own hands a break from a reflexology session!

When practicing dessert techniques, take care not to overwork your hands or arms by applying them for longer than you're comforably able. Sometimes, a particular technique might not feel good to your reflexology buddy. If that's the case, stop doing it and move on to the next technique.

HAND DESSERTS

PULL TECHNIQUE

The pull technique provides a gentle traction to each finger and segment of the hand. While holding the hand at the wrist, grasp the full length of the finger with your working hand and pull gently. **1** At the same time, counter this movement by pulling in the opposite direction at the wrist. Hold for several seconds, and then go on to each finger and the thumb. For another easy hand dessert, simply bend and unbend each finger gently.

SIDE-TO-SIDE

This technique moves the joints of the digits in seldom experienced directions. Position the flats of both of your thumbs and index fingers on either side of your buddy's index finger at the joints. **2** While pushing with the thumb of your right hand, also push with the index finger of your left hand. Do this several times, creating a side-to-side movement of the finger. Move on to each finger and the thumb.

TECHNIQUE

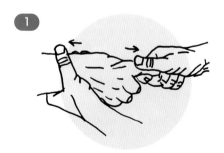

THE WALK-DOWN

The walk-down technique uses thumb walking to stretch the fingers. Hold the hand at the wrist to steady it. With your working hand, place your fingertips on the side of the finger and the flat of your thumb on the other side at the first joint. Now drop your wrist to place the finger in a stretched position. **1** Without moving your fingers, walk down the finger with your thumb by using the thumb-walking technique. Make several passes, then try on each finger.

THE PALM-ROCKER

To relax the whole hand, use the palm-rocker technique. Grasp the person's hand at the knuckles with both of your hands, with the flats of your index and middle fingers on the top and your thumbs on the palm. **2** Simultaneously push with your right thumb and your left fingers, then counter the movement by pushing with your left thumb and right fingers. Do this several times at each of the joints.

TECHNIQUE

1

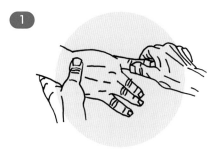

2

THE PALM-LEVER

Further relax your buddy's hand by using the palm-lever technique. With your right hand, grasp the top of the long bone beneath the index finger. With your left hand, grasp the base of this bone. The flats of your thumbs should be resting on the palm. Now push with the fingers of your right hand as you push with the flat of your left thumb. Now switch, pushing with the fingers of your left hand while pushing with the flat of your right thumb.

TECHNIQUE

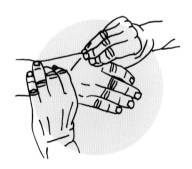

Reflexology Sessions

NOW THAT YOU'VE BECOME ACQUAINTED WITH SOME BASIC SKILLS, it's time to put them together into entire reflexology routines that work each part of the hands. Not only will they rejuvenate the hands, these routines will work each individual reflex area and produce overall relaxation for the entire body.

These sessions begin with desserts to relax the hand, progress through the grip techniques, and then go on to the more advanced walking techniques. If you're focused on affecting reflex areas, note the reflex area being worked. If a part of the hand is particularly sensitive, it might indicate that work in that reflex area is needed. Use the reflexology gloves to better pinpoint these areas. The more often you repeat these workouts, the better your ability will be to notice new areas of the hands that are stressed. If any technique or part of the hand feels particularly good or stressed, remember it for next time—or apply some more work now!

Whole Hand Workout

TIME TO EASE THOSE TIRED HANDS with the whole hand workout. Not only will this routine rejuvenate your reflexology buddy's hands, it will allow you to work each individual reflex area, relaxing the whole body.

The workout begins amd ends with desserts to relax the hand, and works through the grip techniques, focusing primarily on thumb walking to get the most out of your reflexology session. Start by seating your buddy and yourself comfortably, positioned so that you are side by side. Rest the hand on a pillow or folded towel. Make sure to check if there are any areas to be aware of, such as cuts or bruises. Avoid working these areas, and cover cuts with a bandage to avoid touching them. Ready? Let's go!

for a reflexology session focused more on a particular health concern, see the Reflex Areas chapter at the beginning of the book.

WHOLE HAND WORKOUT

DESSERTS

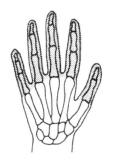

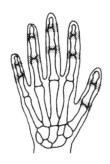

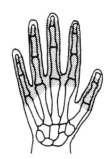

Pull technique (p. 141)

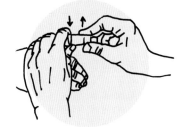

Side-to-side (p. 141)

Walk-down (p. 142)

4

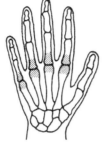

5

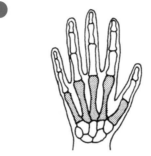

6

Palm-rocker (p. 142)

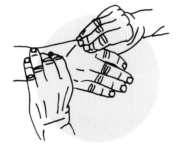

Palm-lever (p. 143)

Single-finger grip on the thumb (p. 123)

Reflex areas: Pituitary gland, Adrenal gland

GRIP TECHNIQUESS *(cont.)*

WALKING TECHNIQUES

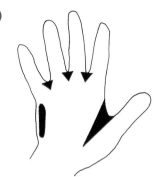

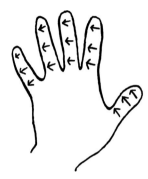

Single-finger grip on the webbing and edge of the hand (p. 122)

Reflex areas: Eye/Ear, Kidney, Arm, Elbow

Multiple-finger grip on the back of the hand (p. 125)

Reflex area: Upper back

Thumb walk on the fingers (p. 132)

Reflex areas: Head/Brain/Sinus, Neck

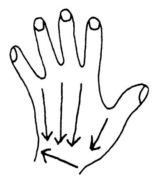

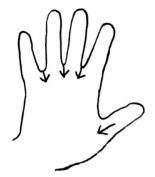

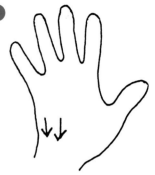

Thumb walk on the upper palm (p. 133)

Reflex areas: Lung, Heart

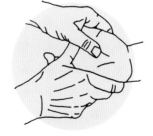

Thumb walk on palm, beginning below the thumb (p. 134)

Reflex areas: Adrenal gland, Pancreas, Kidney, Liver, Gallbladder (right hand), Stomach, Spleen (left hand)

Thumb walk on the heel of the hand (p. 135)

Reflex areas: Small intestines, Colon

WALKING TECHNIQUES *(cont.)*

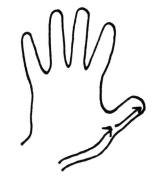

Thumb walk on the edge
of the thumb (p. 138)

Reflex area: Spine

ROTATE ON A POINT

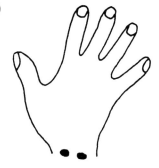

Rotate on a point on the wrist (p. 126)

Reflex areas: Ovary/Testicle,
Uterus/Prostate

WALKING TECHNIQUES

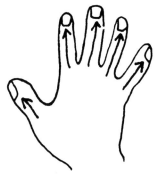

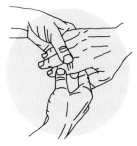

Thumb walk down the backs
of the fingers (p. 137)

Reflex areas: Head, Neck

16

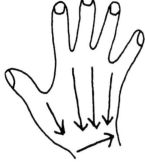

Thumb walk on the top
of the hand (p. 136)

Reflex areas: Upper back,
Lymphatic system

17

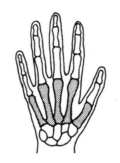

Palm-lever (p. 143)

18

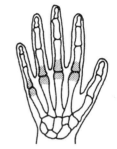

Palm-rocker (p. 142)

DESLATE: *DESSERTS (cont.)*

 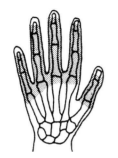

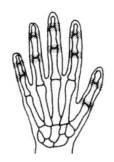

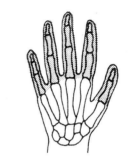

Walk-down (p. 142)

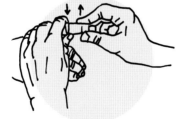

Side-to-side (p. 141)

Pull technique (p. 141)

Index

Notes